A COMMENTARY ON

THE SONG
OF SOLOMON

Tree of Life Bible Commentary
The Song of Solomon
Copyright 1993 by Jon Courson
Jacksonville, OR 97530

Tree of Life Publications
7590 Hwy 238
Jacksonville, OR 97530
Phone: (503) 899-8732
FAX: (503) 899-8068

Library of Congress Catalog Card Number 94-60247
ISBN 1-882743-04-0

All Scripture taken from the King James Version of the Bible.

Printed in the United States of America.

TREE OF LIFE
BIBLE COMMENTARY

THE SONG
OF SOLOMON

JON COURSON

Illustrated by
Lyle Trimmer

CONTENTS

The Song of Solomon —

It was the favorite book of
D.L. Moody, C.H. Spurgeon, and St. John of the Cross.

John Gill, a Puritan preacher, mined 122 sermons from its riches.
Bernard of Clairvaux, a French mystic, brought forth 88 teachings
from Chapter 1 alone.

Solomon wrote 'Vanity of vanities' in Ecclesiastes,
but labeled this book his 'Song of Songs'.
He wrote, 'There is nothing new under the *sun*' in Ecclesiastes,
but wrote of life under the *Son* in his Song.

It's a many-faceted diamond, this glorious Song of Solomon —
for no matter which way it is studied,
or from which angle it is approached,
it is sure to reflect and refract
Jesus Christ —
the Light of the world,
and the Lover of our souls.

Background

THE book before us is one of the most beautiful, but perhaps one of the most controversial books in the entire Bible. It is controversial for two reasons: its content and its intent.

The content of the Song of Solomon is controversial because some see it as nothing more than an erotic Oriental love poem. It was for this reason that Orthodox Jews were not allowed to read it until they were thirty years of age.

But perhaps even more controversial than the content of the Song of Solomon is its intent.

There are those who say it's simply a marriage manual — that in this book a man can learn how to relate to his wife, and a woman can learn how to respond to her husband.

Others say it is an allegory which speaks of Jehovah's love for the nation Israel.

Still others view the Song of Solomon as the account of a love triangle: Solomon representing the world's system, the maiden representing the Church, and the shepherd-king representing Jesus Christ.

But the most commonly held viewpoint, and the one to which I personally ascribe, is that the love between the king and the maiden as seen in the Song of Solomon, is a picture of the love between Jesus and His Church.

Part of the problem in interpreting the Song of Solomon, is that it is not always clear who is speaking. Many translations have added headings of explanation, but as is often the case, they can produce more confusion than clarity. It is therefore necessary to look for contextual clues *within* any given passage to determine whether it is the king or the maiden who is speaking.

In one aspect, this is an extremely difficult book to teach because it is so personal. But I promise you this: Whether you are mystical or analytical by nature, whether you are both, or neither — if you'll spend time quietly and privately with the Lord, reading this book as a love letter from Him — no matter how you choose to interpret it, He will make precious and personal application to your life.

CHAPTER ONE

Song of Solomon 1:1
The song of songs, which is Solomon's.

JESUS is the King of Kings.
>The Temple contained the Holy of Holies.
>>And this is Solomon's Song of Songs.

I Kings 4 tells us that Solomon wrote 1,005 songs, yet this is the only one God saw fit to preserve for eternity.

Song of Solomon 1:2
Let him kiss me with the kisses of his mouth . . .

'Let him kiss me with the kisses of his mouth,' sings the maiden in the opening phrase of Solomon's 'opera'.

When, after realizing he had lived a life of sin and debauchery, the Prodigal returned home, his father greeted him with kisses upon his *neck* (Luke 15:20) — which speak of forgiveness and restoration.

The kisses of the *mouth* here in Song of Solomon, are not the kisses of forgiveness, but the kisses of intimacy and communion.

You cannot kiss two people at one time — don't try it! And one of the things that's so important to understand is, if we desire intimacy with the Lord — not simply the kiss of forgiveness, but the kiss of intimacy — we need to forsake all others. We cannot follow after this idol or that desire, but we must say, 'Lord, I'm fully, completely, totally committed to *You*.'

––––––––––––––––––––

Song of Solomon 1:2
. . . for thy love is better than wine.

Wine speaks of joy. Here, the maiden says to the king, 'Sharing intimacy with you far exceeds even the most joyous substance the world has to offer.'

We've found that to be true, haven't we? When you feel the closeness of the Lord — perhaps at His Table, or in a time when worship is ascending in a powerful way; perhaps when you're walking in the woods or quitely meditating by a lake; perhaps when you're on your knees in your prayer closet or bowing down by your bed — you know that *nothing* compares to His presence.

––––––––––––––––––––

Song of Solomon 1:3
Because of the savour of thy good ointments thy name is as ointment poured forth . . .

When Elvis Presley was popular in the mid-fifties, girls would swoon at the mention of his name. But Jesus' name is much more precious because people don't faint at the name of Jesus — they 'walk and leap and praise God,' (Acts 3:8).

Song of Solomon 1:3
. . . therefore do the virgins love thee.

Any virgin, any person who desires purity and rightness will eventually love Jesus. People often say, 'But Jon, my friend, or my neighbor, or my family member is so good, so pure. Surely he can't go to hell just because he doesn't know Jesus.'

I suggest to you that whoever is truly a spiritual virgin — whoever truly desires goodness and purity and righteousness — will inevitably desire and submit to Jesus Christ.

Conversely, if a person does not want to love the Lord, he is not a good person. That's a hard statement to make, but it's one I believe Scripture backs up through and through.

Truly, 'There is *none* righteous, no, not one. There is none that doeth good,' (Romans 3:10) — but if a person has even a *desire* to be right and pure, he will inevitably follow the Lord.

Song of Solomon 1:4
Draw me, we will run after thee . . .

The maiden says to the king whose name is so precious and whose intimacy she desires,

> 'Unless you draw me,
>> unless you invite me,
>>> unless you reach out to me,
>>>> I can't come.

>> But if you draw me, I will run.'

In John 15, Jesus said, 'You have not chosen Me, but I have chosen you.' You see, we cannot seek after the Lord, unless the Father, through the Spirit, draws and woos us (John 6:44). It's not that we're lazy. It's that we're powerless.

'Draw me, and we will run after thee.' What a prayer to be offered from our lips. 'Draw me, Lord — and as You stir my spirit and pull the strings of my heart, I will come. I will respond. Draw me to You, and I'll run.'

Song of Solomon 1:4
. . . the king hath brought me into his chambers: we will be glad and rejoice in thee, we will remember thy love more than wine: the upright love thee.

Here the scene changes as the maiden is brought into the palace of the king. It is important to understand that before the king became her lover, she was first brought into the palace where she acknowledged him as her lord.

Understand, folks, that you will not experience the intimacy, the warmth, the beauty of a love relationship *with* the Lord until you submit *to* Him as King.

Many people ask me, 'Why don't I feel God's love? Others around me weep and rejoice, but I never feel a thing. Why?'

I answer, 'Perhaps it is because you have not yet come to the palace and truly submitted every part of your personality and being to Him. You see, before there can be intimate communication, there must be complete commitment.'

> Think about it, guys: When you began to date your wife, you couldn't be intimate with her or expressive towards her until there was an absolute commitment made. When you said, 'You are my wife until death do us part,' — the possibility for intimacy became available. Otherwise, it would have been adultery or immorality.
>
> As a man and woman become more committed to each other, they can begin to share more expression. You date a girl, and first you hold her hand. And then you put your arm around her, and then perhaps the goodnight kiss. As the commitment increases, the intimacy can be expressed — but never can be *completely* expressed until you make that lasting commitment, saying, 'You're the one.'

I'm convinced that many times, we don't experience the fulness of intimacy with the Lord because in reality we're still at the 'holding hand' stage with Him. We're not really committed to Him because there are other things and other priorities to which we cling.

We can't experience intimacy until we come into His palace, bow our knee and say, 'You are Lord.'

And that's what's happening here. Before the bride could become intimate with her bridegroom, she first had to be completely submitted to him. It's a very important principle.

Song of Solomon 1:5
I am black . . .

In the presence of the king, the maiden suddenly realizes her own blackness.

Whenever you enter into the company of the Lord, you're in for a shock because you'll be aware of how black you are in and of yourself. That is why when Isaiah came into the Lord's presence, he said, 'Woe is me. I am unclean. I am undone,' (Isaiah 6:5).

You cannot be proud or boastful; you cannot be self-assured in the presence of the Lord. You might think you're pretty together now, but when you come into His presence and you see *His* beauty, *His* holiness, *His* loveliness — you say, 'Woe is me. I am black.'

Song of Solomon 1:5
. . . but comely O ye daughters of Jerusalem . . .

I'm black, but I'm also comely because I'm in Christ Jesus. He has cleansed me with His blood. He has put me on His team. He has made me a part of His Bride and Body. He has robed me with His righteousness. I'm black; but I am comely because of what He has done for me.

Song of Solomon 1:5
. . . as the tents of Kedar, as the curtains of Solomon.

The tents of Kedar were black tents, made of black goats' hair. The curtains of Solomon were made of white linen.

'I know I'm black on the outside,' the maiden says, 'but I also know I'm pure.'

It's this dichotomy, this struggle of which each of us is aware. Like Paul, we know that in our flesh dwells no good thing (Romans 7:18). And yet, like Paul, we have the treasure of the Lord's presence within our earthen vessels (II Corinthians 4:7).

Song of Solomon 1:6
Look not upon me, because I am black, because the sun hath looked upon me: my mother's children were angry with me; they made me the keeper of the vineyards; but mine own vineyard have I not kept.

Here the maiden explains why she's black. Instead of just saying, 'I'm black but comely,' and leaving it at that, she gives a reason for why she's black.

Do you ever do that?

Do you ever say,

> 'If you had parents like I had, you would be black, too,' or
> 'If you had a boss like I do, you would understand,' or
> 'If you had a husband like I have, you would be *really* dark'?

She says, 'The reason I'm so tan' — which was totally looked down upon in her culture — 'is because my background was harsh and my brothers were hostile. The sun came down upon me. My brothers made me take care of all of the vineyards. I had to work outside — and that's why I am the way that I am.'

Oh, how often today we hear people say, 'The reason I am the way that I am is because of my brothers . . . or my mother . . . .'

Don't do that. You don't need to explain why you're black. Just admit that you are!

Song of Solomon 1:7
Tell me, O thou whom my soul loveth, where thou feedest, where thou makest thy flock to rest at noon: for why should I be as one that turneth aside by the flocks of thy companions?

Perhaps realizing that she didn't need to be defensive about her blackness, the bride changes the subject. She says, 'Tell me where you keep your flocks.'

Here the bride shows us that her king is also a shepherd. This is why some people say there are three main characters in this story. The shepherd could not be the king, they reason, for what king is a shepherd?

Oh, but there *is* a King Who is a Shepherd: Jesus Christ — the King of Kings and the Shepherd of our souls —

> the Good Shepherd (John 10:14),
> the Great Shepherd (Hebrews 13:20),
> the Chief Shepherd (I Peter 5:4).

'Tell me,' says the bride to her shepherd-king, 'where do you keep your flocks? I want to be there too. Why should I settle for your companions when I can have you? I want to be with *you*. Where are you?'

I feel that in my heart. Sometimes I say, 'Lord, where are You? I don't want to settle for just spending time with Your companions. I want You, Lord. Oh, I appreciate the advice of my brothers and sisters — but I need *You*, Lord.'

Do you ever feel like you just need to be with the Lord — and you wonder where He is? 'Where are You, Lord? In the noon day — when the sun is highest and the heat is hottest — where can I find You, Lord?'

Notice the king's answer . . .

Song of Solomon 1:8
If thou know not, O thou fairest among women, go thy way forth by the footsteps of the flock . . .

9

'Do you want to know where I am? Do you want to be with me? Do you want to know where I hang out in the heat of the day, in the hot times?' asks the king. 'I'll tell you: First, follow the flock.'

If you want to find the Lord and know the Lord — follow His flock. There is no room for the 'Lone Ranger' mentality in the Body of Christ which says, 'I don't need Church. I don't need Bible Study. I don't need Communion. I've grown beyond those things. It's just me and Jesus.'

I have yet to see a Christian who, over the long haul, has done well as a Lone Ranger. It doesn't work. The Bible says,

> And let us consider one another to provoke unto love and to good works: not forsaking the assembling of ourselves together, as the manner of some is; but exhorting one another: and so much the more, as ye see the day approaching.
>
> Hebrews 10:25

We need to follow the flock, to be a part of the flock. The Lord designed it that way. He's building a *family* — living stones being fit together for a holy priesthood (II Peter 2:5).

Song of Solomon 1:8
. . . and feed thy kids beside the shepherds' tents.

'Secondly, ' said the king, 'feed the kids. Find those who are young and feed them. That's where you'll find me.'

Saints, when you feel like you don't know where the Lord is during the heat of the day, during the hard times in your life — come to church. Find some new Christians — some young believers, some Sunday school kids, some junior highers — and feed them. It's *so* important.

I just returned from camp Monday night, where I taught our 4th, 5th, and 6th graders. Nine or ten opened their hearts to receive Jesus. What a joy!

The counsellors were hyped. In a counsellors' meeting, many of them shared that, due to full schedules and obligations, they weren't sure they wanted to be there initially — but once they began 'feeding the kids', there was no place they'd rather be.

That's always the way it is. Once you're 'feeding kids' — whether in a home Bible study, a Sunday School class, or discipling someone one-on-one — you experience the flow of God's love through you to someone else, and it's wonderful!

Where is the Lord? Follow the flock, feed the kids, and I promise you will find Him and experience Him in special ways.

Song of Solomon 1:9
I have compared thee, O my love, to a company of horses in Pharaoh's chariots.

The king doesn't compare the maiden to a donkey or to a beast of burden. He compares her to a horse — a prized possession in that culture.

In other words, he says, 'I have compared you to a Ferrari. I have compared you to a BMW. You're something special.'

Notice this key concept as you read through this book: The king has only good things to say about this woman who recognizes her own blackness.

So too with us. Jesus looks at us and is in love with *us*! I am so aware of my blackness, yet Jesus actually desires *me*. *Great* is the mystery!

Song of Solomon 1:10
Thy cheeks are comely with rows of jewels . . .

How can cheeks have rows of jewels?

Women in Solomon's day wore headdresses with jewels connected to them by leather straps that hung down upon their cheeks.

Song of Solomon 1:10
. . . thy neck with chains of gold.

Gold is the metal of monarchy.

Song of Solomon 1:11
We will make thee borders [braids] of gold . . .

Who is 'we?' I believe this speaks of the Trinity. 'We will make thee braids of gold. We're only going to make you *more* beautiful,' the Lord says.

How is gold braided?
By pounding and beating it.

Sometimes we wonder what the Lord is doing in our lives. He is refining us and beautifying us even through pounding and beating. When we wonder what the Lord is doing during the times of trial and testing, He is braiding us — His gold — through hard times of pounding and beating and shaping.

'What right does He have to pound on me and to beautify me in that way?' you ask.

Read on.

Song of Solomon 1:11
. . . with studs of silver.

Silver is the metal of redemption.

Jesus redeemed you. He bought you with His blood. Therefore, He can beautify you as He sees fit.

Song of Solomon 1:12
While the king sitteth at his table . . .

I Kings 4 says that at Solomon's table every day there were thirty measures (190 bushels) of fine four, threescore measures (390 bushels) of meal, ten fat oxen, 20 oxen out of pasture, 100 sheep besides harts, roebucks, fallow deer, and fatted fowl. Solomon's table was abundant in provision.

Song of Solomon 1:12
. . . my spikenard sendeth from the smell thereof.

It was when the maiden sat at the table of her shepherd-king that the fragrance came forth from her.

Folks, when you feast at the Lord's table, a fragrance comes forth. Jesus said, 'This do in remembrance of Me,' (Luke 22:19), and yet we as believers so often say, 'We don't have time, or the inclination, or the desire to come to the Communion Table.'

When you feast at the Lord's Table, it's a fragrant, beautiful expression of love in His sight. Please don't come to church only to get. Don't come Sunday nights just to see if you can be blessed. We assemble together because it's fragrant to *Him*. The Lord is blessed when He sees His kids remember Him. How it changed my understanding of Church when I understood that I wasn't coming just to get. I was coming to honor my Lord.

The bride says, 'At the king's table, the fragrance of spikenard emanated from me.'

What is spikenard?

It's the same ointment Mary released upon Jesus as she broke the alabaster box. Jesus said, 'She has done this as a memorial unto Me. And this shall be spoken of wherever the Gospel is preached. Disciples, leave her alone. This is a beautiful act,' (Mark 14:3-9).

Spikenard was released upon Jesus.
Spikenard is going forth at the king's table.
Spikenard is the way you can bless Jesus today.
At His Table, spikenard flows.

Song of Solomon 1:13
A bundle of myrrh is my well-beloved unto me . . .

We are all born and will die. It's a matter of how we live, that varies.

What is myrrh?
A burial spice.

Even at Jesus' birth, as He was wrapped in swaddling clothes and later presented with myrrh, a statement was being made that He was born to die.

Song of Solomon 1:13
. . . he shall lie all night betwixt my breasts.

This passage is better translated: '*it* shall lie all night betwixt my breasts,' referring to the bundle of myrrh.

Who is the person who is really in love with the Lord, the person who feels the presence of the Lord upon his breast, and within his heart?

It is the person who understands that the Lord died for him personally and for those sins which are so black. It is the person who realizes that Christ's death is not just theology — but reality. It is the person who says,

'I'm a sinner. And the Lord died for me. It's not just the teachings He shared or the life He lived — it's what He did on Calvary that makes me love Him.'

It is the person who remembers the Cross.

———————————

Song of Solomon 1:14
My beloved is unto me as a cluster of camphire in the vineyards of Engedi.

En-gedi is a beautiful oasis surrounded by the deserts of the the Dead Sea. It's where David hung out when he fled from Saul — a refreshing spot, a precious spot.

Here, the maiden says to her king, 'You're an oasis to me. You're like the camphire — or the cypress tree. The shade tree, the beauty in this desert-dry world — that's what you are to me.'

———————————

Song of Solomon 1:15
Behold, thou art fair, my love; behold, thou art fair . . .

The king replies, 'You are fair.' 'Fair' does not mean 'adequate', 'OK', or 'passable'. It means 'excellent', 'ravishing', 'wonderful'.

Song of Solomon 1:15
. . . thou hast doves' eyes.

The eyes reveal what is in the soul. The dove being a symbol of the Holy Spirit, this verse says that Jesus sees His Spirit in my soul. He doesn't see me in my flesh and stupidity — which is obvious to many. He sees the reality of His life being lived through mine.

And He says to every one of you who know Him, to every single one of you who is a believer, 'You are fair. You're wonderful — because I see in you My work and My life.'

Gang, *everything* the king says to his maiden is positive and encouraging. And that's the way the Lord sees us.

Song of Solomon 1:16
Behold, thou art fair, my beloved, yea, pleasant: also our bed is green.

The maiden says, *'You're* pleasant, lord. It's not me. It's you!'

Now, remember that in verse 7, the maiden asked for two things: that she might be fed and that she might have rest.

What does she find?

She is fed when she sits at his table in verse 12.
And here in verse 16, she finds rest in his house.

Song of Solomon 1:16
The beams of our house are cedar, and our rafters of fir.

The rest the maiden found in the house of her king was not some shaky, fragile place that would collapse or cave in if she messed up. It was girded with beams of cedar and rafters of fir.

'King,' she says, 'I'm safe here — not because of who I am, but because of what you've done.' The bride rejoices in the fact that she could be at rest in the palace of the king.

I do the same. I'm at rest tonight because of what Jesus has done for me.

CHAPTER TWO

Song of Solomon 2:1
I am the rose of Sharon,

AS Chapter Two opens, the shepherd-king speaks, saying, 'I am the rose of Sharon.'

Jesus identified Himself as the Bread of Life (John 6:35) and the Light of the world (John 8:12). But here, He's speaking of something more than an essential need or provision for life. Jesus is saying, 'I'm not just Bread and Light — I'm something beautiful to behold. I don't only give you the essentials — I bring beauty to your life.'

Song of Solomon 2:1
. . . and the lily of the valleys.

When Jesus says, 'I'm a lily,' in our society we think, 'Pansy.' But Jesus Christ was no pansy.

A carpenter before there were Skil saws and power tools, I suggest to you He had massive arms.

Not one vendor dared challenge Him when He overturned money stands and drove out cattle in the Temple (Matthew 21:12).

When He was taken to the edge of a cliff and about to be thrown over the edge by an angry mob, it took only a look from Him to part the crowd (Luke 4:29-30).

Yet at the same time, Jesus isn't a 'Clint Eastwood' type. I'm so glad the Lord isn't like Clint Eastwood! Wouldn't it be disappointing to get to heaven and hear Him say, 'Make My Day'?

This One Who is the essence of masculinity is also oh, so tender and beautiful. He says, 'I am the Rose of Sharon and the lily of the valley.'

Song of Solomon 2:2
As the lily among thorns, so is my love among the daughters.

The king speaks of the maiden, saying, 'I am a lily, and you're like me. As the lily among thorns, I see you and I love the beauty I see in you.'

Song of Solomon 2:3
As the apple tree among the trees of the wood, so is my beloved among the sons. I sat down under his shadow with great delight, and his fruit was sweet to my taste.

The maiden praises the pleasantness of her king.

In Van Wey's Market a couple days ago, Fred gave me a yellow and red apple and said, 'This apple is from New Zealand. Take a bite.' I wouldn't normally have bought such a different-looking apple, but I bit into it — and it was great!

That's the way it is with the Lord. Psalm 34 says, 'Oh, taste and see that the Lord is good.' You'll never know how sweet Jesus is until you taste of Him. Give the Lord a chance tomorrow morning. Give the Lord a chance this evening. Taste and see. Spend time with Him in the shade of His presence, eating of His fruit.

Song of Solomon 2:4-6
He brought me to the banqueting house, and his banner over me was love. Stay me with flagons, comfort me with apples: for I am sick of love. His left hand is under my head, and his right hand doth embrace me.

The king's banner over the maiden was not, 'Get it Together', or 'Try A Little Harder'.

It was 'I Love You'.

Most of us think that if we sat down under the Lord's tree and ate of His fruit, He would say, 'At last I've got you. Now I can give you a piece of My mind.'

But that's not the heart of the Lord, for there is *no* condemnation to them that are in Christ Jesus (Romans 8:1). His left hand is able to support you. His right hand is ready to embrace you. And His banner over you is Love.

Song of Solomon 2:7
I charge you, O ye daughters of Jerusalem, by the roes, and by the hinds of the field . . .

Here, the king speaks to a group of women who have appeared on stage. The daughters of Jerusalem, seen throughout the story, seem to be meddlers — coming on the scene every now and then to give observation and input.

Some Christians are like the daughters of Jerusalem. They pop in every once in awhile to tell you what they think you should be doing, or why you're not together.

Song of Solomon 2:7
. . . that ye stir not up, nor awake my love, till he please.

A better translation would be '. . . that ye stir not up, nor awake my love, till *I* please.'

'Mind your own business,' the king said. 'Don't wake her up. I want her to be at rest.'

What a good word for the 'daughter of Jerusalem' in each of us. Listen to the word of the King: 'Mind your own business. Let My children sleep until *I* please. *I'll* take care of them. *I* will awaken them. You busybodies, back off.'

How I thank the Lord that He lets me rest in Him. In the only autobiographical statement Jesus ever made, He said, 'I am meek and lowly and you shall find *rest* in your souls,' (Matthew 11:29). The only thing Jesus said about Himself was, 'I am meek and lowly — not harsh and demanding. Walk with Me, learn of Me, and you shall find rest in your soul.'

Song of Solomon 2:8
The voice of my beloved . . .

Here, the story takes on a new dimension. After a night of intimacy between the king and his beloved, the bride hears the voice of her shepherd-king before the breaking of the dawn.

Song of Solomon 2:8
. . . behold, he cometh leaping upon the mountains, skipping
upon the hills.

While she remains in bed, she hears the voice of her beloved as he leaps on the mountains and skips on the hills. Scripturally, mountains are often symbolic of problems. And here the shepherd-king, a picture of Jesus Christ, leaps on the mountains and skips on the hills.

I like that! The problems which seem so overwhelming to us, the obstacles which seem so awesome to us — are mere stepping stones to the Lord.

A woman once asked me, 'Isn't my problem too small to bring to the Lord?'

I asked her in return, 'Is there any problem that's *big* to the Lord?'

The problems which seem so big to us shrink in light of the Lord's power, might, and awesome size.

———————————

Song of Solomon 2:9
My beloved is like a roe or a young hart: behold, he standeth behind our wall, he looketh forth at the windows, shewing himself through the lattice.

The bride remains in the room, while her love is outside leaping on mountains and skipping over hills. She feels secure and safe — and yet, they are separated. She is inside — 'into herself' if you would — while her love is outside calling to her.

———————————

Song of Solomon 2:10-12
My beloved spake, and said unto me, Rise up, my love, my fair one, and come away. For, lo, the winter is past, the rain is over and gone; The flowers appear on the earth; the time of the singing of birds is come, and the voice of the turtle (dove) is heard in our land;

Before the dawn breaks, the shepherd-king stands outside the window and says to his bride,

'Come! There are places to go and things to do. A new season is upon us. New opportunities are before us. Arise. Come away. Let's go!'

Song of Solomon 2:13
The fig tree putteth forth her green figs, and the vines with the tender grape give a good smell. Arise, my love, my fair one, and come away.

Throughout Scripture, the fig tree is symbolic of the nation Israel. In Matthew 24, Jesus said that the budding forth of the nation Israel would be a sign that His coming is nigh. He went on to say that the generation that sees Israel blossom would not pass away. It would be the final generation (Matthew 24:34).

We are that generation, folks, for in 1948, Israel began to bloom. Thus, I hear the voice of our Shepherd-King saying to us,

'Arise, Church! Get out of bed.
    There are places to go;
        things to do;
            countries to reach;
                tasks before you in these last days.'

Song of Solomon 2:14
O my dove, that art in the clefts of the rock, in the secret
places of the stairs, let me see thy countenance, let me hear
thy voice; for sweet is thy voice, and thy countenance is
comely.

The bride is still speaking, quoting the words of the shepherd-king.

Why was the countenance of the bride comely?
Because she was in the clefts of the rock.

> Moses desired to see the presence, the glory, the reality of God. God
> answered his request by saying, 'No man can see Me and live. But
> I'll tell you what I'll do: Hide in the cleft, or the crevice of the rock,
> Moses, and I'll put My hand over you as I pass by. Then I'll remove
> My hand and allow you to see My afterglow,' (Genesis 33:13-23).

The only way we can see God, walk with God and have fellowship with
God is if, like Moses, we are hid in the cleft of the Rock. And, as the
Apostle Paul said, that Rock is Christ (I Corinthians 10:4).

Listen, gang. We are comely not because of *who* we are, but because of *where*
we are. We are *in* the Rock. We are *in* Christ Jesus. That's why you can say
with absolute certainty and integrity, 'I am comely. I am spiritually
beautiful because I am hidden in Christ Jesus — surrounded and covered
by *His* righteousness. In me, dwells no good thing. I know that I'm black —
and yet I'm in the cleft of the Rock.'

> Suppose the ushers gave each of you a Haagen Dazs bar when you
> came in the door — with the instructions to eat it immediately.
> When I stood up to teach, I wouldn't see any of those Haagen Dazs

bars because they would be *in* you — covered by layer after layer of you. Totally surrounded, enveloped, lost in your mass!

That's exactly what happens when you become a Christian. Not only does Jesus Christ come in you, but you are in Christ Jesus. What a fabulous, truth that is. When you see it, you will be liberated and gloriously free!

Song of Solomon 2:15
Take us the foxes, the little foxes, that spoil the vines: for our vines have tender grapes.

The king speaks. Remember the context: the morning is about to break. He stands outside the window of his bride and says, 'Come away my beloved. There are places to go and things to do. You're like a dove — hid in the cleft of the rock. You're comely.' But then he adds, 'Watch out for the little foxes.'

In that day, vineyards were surrounded by stone walls to keep the animals from destroying the grapes. But little foxes would find a way to weasel through the crevices and gnaw on the tender vines within.

What is the shepherd-king saying?

He's saying to his love, to his bride, 'Watch out for the little foxes — those subtle things that will sneak in, gnaw on the vine, and destroy your fruit.'

It was a word of warning to the bride, but she didn't catch it, for watch what happens next . . .

Song of Solomon 2:16-17
My beloved is mine, and I am his: he feedeth among the lilies.
Until the day break, and the shadows flee away, turn, my
beloved, and be thou like a roe or young hart upon the
mountains of Bether.

The bride didn't heed the warning of her beloved, nor did she respond to his invitation. Rather, she rolled over in bed and said, 'My beloved is mine. I'm safe in the position that I have, secure in our relationship — so go ahead, shepherd-king. Go ahead and keep running on top of the mountains, skipping over hills — and I'll see you later in the day.'

How indicting! How much that's like me. The Lord wakens me sometimes before the day begins to break, and my natural inclination is to say,

> 'Oh, Lord, I'm so thankful You're mine — it's so neat being linked
> to Your grace, Your mercy, Your lovingkindness. Go ahead and
> run on the mountains, and I'll be with You in a little bit.'

When it's dark outside or cold inside, when you have been up late the night before, or have a full day ahead, how easy it is to roll over and take a rain check on the Lord's invitation to rise up. There are things He desires to say, revelation He desires to give, places He desires to take us — but so often we're like the bride as we say, 'I'm so thankful that You're mine, Lord. I'll see You later.'

That's a dangerous thing to do. For, as the bride will discover, by the time she rises, her shepherd-king will be gone.

CHAPTER THREE

Song of Solomon 3:1
By night on my bed I sought him whom my soul loveth: I
sought him, but I found him not.

THE bride sought her shepherd-king, but couldn't find him because she had missed the moment when he had given an invitation for her to come into spectacular territory with Him. Now it's night and she's alone, wondering, 'Where is he?'

Have you ever had that experience? Have you ever wondered, 'Where's the Lord? What's happening? What's going on? Could it be that when I told Him to go away as I turned over and buried my face in the pillow, He took me up on it?'

When Brett and I went skydiving a few months ago, one of the things that we were told very, very pointedly was that there was a moment when we *had* to jump. If we didn't jump at that time, we would miss the landing spot altogether.

A skydiver must jump when the instructor says, 'Jump!' A hang glider has to take off when the current is right. A surfer needs to hit the waves when the sets are coming in.

There are certain things we *cannot* postpone. And many of us are learning that one of them is responding to the voice of the Lord when we hear Him say, 'Arise, come away. I've got some things I want to talk to you about.'

It might be a Saturday afternoon, a Tuesday evening, or an early Thursday morning. Whenever it is — respond to the Lord's invitation, or you'll miss an incredible moment.

Song of Solomon 3:2
I will rise now, and go about the city in the streets, and in the broad ways I will seek him whom my soul loveth: I sought him, but I found him not.

Sometimes our Love — our Lord — allows us to search and seek for awhile before He makes Himself known to us again.

Is He playing hard to get?
Not at all.

He's teaching us not to take our relationship with Him for granted. If we do, we'll become involved with and vulnerable to things which are destructive and detrimental. And so the Lord, our Love, our Shepherd-King says to us, 'Sometimes I will hide Myself from you for a season so that you won't take for granted the relationship which I've cultivated with you.'

Song of Solomon 3:3
The watchmen that go about the city found me: to whom I
said, Saw ye him whom my soul loveth?

The watchmen were unable to help the bride locate her lord. In Scripture, watchmen are symbolic of those watching over the city. They're leaders. And yet they were unable to help her.

Sometimes we think, 'If I could just get some counselling, if I could just get some help from a leader, then I could find the Lord once again.' That's not necessarily the case. You need to seek the Lord *personally*.

'And ye shall seek Me, and find Me, when ye shall search for Me with all your heart,' (Jeremiah 29:13), saith the Lord. It's when you are serious about seeking the Lord *yourself* that you will find Him.

Song of Solomon 3:4
It was but a little that I passed from them, but I found him
whom my soul loveth: I held him, and would not let him go,
until I had brought him into my mother's house, and into the
chamber of her that conceived me.

When the bride finds her shepherd-king, she doesn't wait to bring him across town to their house, but takes the first opportunity possible and the first place available to be with him privately.

I like that! It's always a blessing when I see people out on the grounds — in the amphitheatre, under a tree, or up on the hill — seeking God. They're not waiting for a Sunday service or a Wednesday study. They're just seeking the Lord even on a Tuesday.

Whether you come here, or go to the park; whether you stay in your backyard, or in your car — the point is: Don't wait!

The bride didn't. She grabbed her love and took him into her mother's home, which was evidently near to where she found him.

Song of Solomon 3:5
I charge you, O ye daughters of Jerusalem, by the roes, and by the hinds of the field, that ye stir not up, nor awake my love, till he please.

The word 'he' is better translated 'I'. Thus, the king says to the daughters of Jerusalem,

'Don't bother her.
Let her rest.

Don't interrogate her.
Let her rest.

Don't judge her.
Let her rest.

She's my bride and I have ordained rest and sleep for her.'

It's often the tendency of the daughters of Jerusalem to show up on the scene and say,

'Well, why didn't you respond to his calling in the first place? Why did you let him go? What's going on in your life?'

And yet the king says to those daughters, 'Don't judge her. Let her rest.'

I believe the King says that to us today:

> 'Don't judge him. Don't judge her. Leave it to *Me* to deal with them in the right way, at the perfect time.'

Song of Solomon 3:6
Who is this that cometh out of the wilderness like pillars of smoke, perfumed with myrrh and frankincense, with all powders of the merchant?

The scene changes. As the bride is brought out of the wilderness, escorted by the king's soldiers and carried upon his bed, a company of maidens asks, 'Who is this one coming out of the wilderness who smells of frankincense and myrrh?'

Guess who it is.
It's us!

We have been loved by the Lord. He has brought us out of the wilderness of sin, has given us rest in Him, and we have begun to take on *His* fragrance.

Song of Solomon 3:7-10
Behold his bed, which is Solomon's; threescore valiant men are about it, of the valiant of Israel. They all hold swords, being expert in war: every man hath his sword upon his thigh

because of fear in the night. King Solomon made himself a chariot of the wood of Lebanon. He made the pillars thereof of silver, the bottom thereof of gold, the covering of it of purple, the midst thereof being paved with love, for the daughters of Jerusalem.

The maidens marvel as they watch the bride being escorted on a glorious bed, surrounded by soldiers with swords strapped to their thighs.

Who are the threescore valiant men surrounding the bride, marching under orders of the king?

I believe they're angels — 'ministering spirits' as Hebrews 1:14 calls them — who have been sent to escort us out of the wilderness.

You are surrounded by angels. Not only does the Spirit live *inside* of you, but there are angels travelling *alongside* of you: incredible creatures who are so powerful that it only takes *one* to hold *all* of the demons captive in the abyss (Revelation 9:11).

Song of Solomon 3:11
Go forth, O ye daughters of Zion, and behold king Solomon with the crown wherewith his mother crowned him in the day of his espousals, and in the day of the gladness of his heart.

In other words, the maiden says to the daughters of Jersualem, 'Check out the king!'

Most of us believe that Jesus loves us generically.
But the message of Solomon's Song is that
Jesus loves us individually
and is in love with us radically.

CHAPTER FOUR

Song of Solomon 4:1
Behold, thou art fair, my love; behold, thou art fair . . .

'THOU art fair,' says the king to his bride. As we saw in Chapter 1, fair doesn't mean 'adequate' — it means 'excellent'.

And as the king views his bride, so the King of Kings views us, His Church. Gang, Jesus does not look at you and say,

> 'I love you, but . . . .'
> 'I'll love you if . . . .'
> 'I'll love you when . . . .'

He says,

> 'I love you — period.'

Most of us believe that Jesus loves us generically. But that's not the message of this book. Solomon's message to us is that Jesus loves us individually and is in love with us radically.

Song of Solomon 4:1
. . . thou hast doves' eyes within thy locks . . .

I got a letter yesterday from a guy who said, 'I've been listening to a fellow named Garner Ted Armstrong on the radio. Although I've only been a Christian for three months, something about him doesn't ring true.'

I wrote him back and said, 'That's great! Even though you can't quote chapter and verse at this point in your walk, you have doves' eyes — you have Holy Spirit discernment. You see things others don't see. You understand things others don't understand, for the Holy Spirit lives inside you.'

Concerning those who would seduce you, the apostle John said, 'The anointing which ye have received of him abideth in you, and ye need not that any man teach you, but as the same anointing teacheth you of all things . . . .' (I John 2:27).

In other words, when someone knocks on your door, preaches on TV, or talks to you at work, you'll know in your heart if things aren't right. You have doves' eyes. The Holy Spirit will give you discernment. Jesus said, 'When the Spirit comes, He will guide you into all truth,' (John 16:13). I'm so thankful for the Holy Spirit. How I need His private tutoring!

Song of Solomon 4:1
. . . thy hair is as a flock of goats, that appear from mount Gilead.

Scripturally, hair is symbolic of two things: consecration and submission.

The Nazarites — those who were *consecrated* to the things of the Lord — were not to cut their hair. That is why Samson was not to cut his hair. He was to have been a Nazarite all his life (Judges 13:5).

Paul wrote that long hair is a sign that a woman is *submitted* to her husband, and that she has placed herself under his covering (I Corinthians 11:15).

Song of Solomon 4:2
Thy teeth are like a flock of sheep that are even shorn, which came up from the washing; whereof every one bear twins, and none is barren among them.

Biblically, teeth speak of our ability to appropriate and assimilate truth. As we mature in our walk with the Lord, we are able to bite into more meaty subjects with greater understanding (Hebrews 5:12-14).

Song of Solomon 4:3
Thy lips are like a thread of scarlet, and thy speech is comely . . .

The prophet Isaiah said, 'My lips are unclean,' (Isaiah 6:5). All of us are aware that our lips, symbolic of our speech, are often polluted or defiled. And yet, positionally, our King looks at us and says, 'Your lips are like scarlet. Because they are washed in My blood, your sins and iniquities will I remember no more,' (Jeremiah 31:34).

Song of Solomon 4:3
. . . thy temples are like a piece of a pomegranate within thy
locks.

The temple speaks of our thought life. The king says to his bride, 'Your thoughts are like pomegranates — fruitful and good.'

As Paul wrote to the Philippians, we are to be thinking about whatever things are true, honest, just, pure, lovely, of good report, virtuous, and praiseworthy (Philippians 4:8) — fruitful thoughts, good thoughts, productive thoughts.

Song of Solomon 4:4
Thy neck is like the tower of David builded for an armoury,
whereon there hang a thousand bucklers, all shields of mighty
men.

This speaks of serenity, of tranquility, of peace. You see, in Solomon's day, the tower of David, built atop Mt. Zion in the city of Jerusalem, could be seen for miles. Shields hanging on the tower of David signified peace. When the shields were gone, however, it meant battle was breaking out somewhere.

Thus, when the king says, 'Your neck is like the tower of David with shields hung thereon,' he was saying, 'There's a serenity and a peacefulness about you which I find attractive and restful.'

Song of Solomon 4:5-7
Thy two breasts are like two young roes that are twins, which feed among the lilies. Until the day break, and the shadows flee away, I will get me to the mountain of myrrh, and to the hill of frankincense. Thou art all fair, my love; there is no spot in thee.

'No spot in thee?' You may be saying,

> 'That might be true of the maiden, but not of me. If you're talking about tranquility and serenity, speech that is comely, thoughts that are fruitful, eyes that are pure — you're not talking about *me*.'

Yes it *is* you. That's what this book is for — that you might see yourself the way the Lord sees you. We are so aware of our blackness, our faults, our shortcomings. And we are *certainly* aware of everyone else's blackness and faults and shortcomings!

But how does the Lord view His Bride?
Through the filter of His blood.

That is, His blood takes away all sin, defilement, and iniquity positionally. As He looks at you, He approves of you; He's in love with you; and He is pleased to be linked to you for all eternity.

That's the message of this book. One of the primary purposes of the Song of Solomon is that you will see yourself as the Lord sees you.

That means when the Lord calls us, saying,
'Pray.
Worship.
Witness.
Walk with Me,'

we can block out that little voice which says,

'You can't pray. You can't worship. You can't witness. You can't walk with the Lord because you're all spotted and black, messed up and ugly. You're gross. You're out of it. You're sick.'

Do you ever hear those kinds of voices?

That's the accuser of the brethren who accuses us day and night (Revelation 12:10).

What does the Lord say?
He says,

'You're lovely. I approve of everything about you. I not only have compassion *on* you, but I have passion *for* you. I am really impressed and blessed by you.'

If you can grab this and live in it, your walk with the Lord will be so free, so beautiful. Again, I don't mean to be redundant, but in Chapter 1, the maiden said, 'I am black,' and gave reasons or excuses for her blackness. Here, however, she's beginning to learn just to relax and rest in the perspective that her shepherd-king has of her.

Song of Solomon 4:8-9
Come with me from Lebanon, my spouse, with me from Lebanon: look from the top of Amana, from the top of Shenir and Hermon, from the lions' dens, from the mountains of the leopards. Thou hast ravished my heart, my sister, my spouse;

thou hast ravished my heart with one of thine eyes, with one chain of thy neck.

I love this passage because it once again demonstrates that our God is the God of the Second Chance. The first time the shepherd-king said to his bride, 'Come, let's go up on the mountains,' she put him off and lost the moment.

But guess what the king does. He comes back and says, 'Let's go for it' again.

The Lord gives us chance after chance after chance. He doesn't
>write us off His list,
>>take us out of the game,
>>>cut us from the team,
>>>>divorce us,
>>>>>or forget about us.

He says,

'I'll give you another chance, Bride. Let's go to the top of the mountains.'

Song of Solomon 4:10
How fair is thy love, my sister, my spouse! how much better is thy love than wine! and the smell of thine ointments than all spices!

In Chapter 1, the bride said to her king, 'Your love is better than wine.'

But here in Chapter 4, he says to her, 'How *much* better is thy love than wine,' which, in Hebrew, meant his love for her *greatly* exceeded her love for him.

What does that say to me?

It says that at the moment when I love my Lord the most — when perhaps I'm moved to tears or brought to complete silence, deeply touched and very impressed — my love for Him can't compare to His love for me.

The Apostle John wrote, 'We love Him because He first loved us,' (I John 4:19). His love for you is much more intense than your love for Him even at the most intense moment you have ever experienced. There's passion in the heart of the Lord for *you*. You are His Bride.

Song of Solomon 4:11
Thy lips, O my spouse, drop as the honeycomb: honey and milk are under thy tongue; and the smell of thy garments is like the smell of Lebanon.

'Your language is as sweet as honey, as sustaining and strengthening as milk,' says the shepherd-king.

Song of Solomon 4:12
A garden enclosed is my sister, my spouse; a spring shut up, a fountain sealed.

Every king in Solomon's time had a private garden wherein he would find cool refuge in the heat of the day.

So too, you are a garden created for your Lord's pleasure. He desires to walk in the garden of your life, to partake of the fruit which He has planted, to savor the fragrances which He has instilled, to enjoy the work which He has wrought in you. You are created for Him, and He wants not only to work in your life, but to walk in your garden.

Before man fell, God walked with Adam in the cool of the day. So too, when the sun sets this evening, the Lord will be waiting for you, longing for you, desiring to walk with you. And when the dawn breaks tomorrow morning, He will be there again.

Song of Solomon 4:13-14
Thy plants are an orchard of pomegranates, with pleasant fruits; camphire, with spikenard, Spikenard and saffron; calamus and cinnamon, with all trees of frankincense; myrrh and aloes, with all the chief spices:

These are all sweet spices. 'You are my garden,' said the king. Everything about you is sweet to my senses and in you I find refuge, rest, refreshment.'

Song of Solomon 4:15
A fountain of gardens, a well of living waters, and streams from Lebanon.

What made the garden of the bride so fruitful?
A well of living waters.

> Jesus stood and cried, saying, If any man thirst, let him come unto me, and drink. He that believeth on me, as the scripture hath said, out of his belly shall flow rivers of living water. (But this spake he of the Spirit, which they that believe on him should receive: for the Holy Ghost was not yet given; because that Jesus was not yet glorified.)
>
> John 7:37-39

What makes you fruitful and refreshing, prolific and productive?
The flowing of the Holy Ghost within and from your life.

Seek the blessing of the Holy Spirit. Jesus taught us to ask the Father for the blessing of the Holy Ghost (Luke 11:13), for when the Holy Spirit flows *in* you and *through* you, there is a fruitfulness *about* you. Without Him, there's a barrenness and a dryness.

Song of Solomon 4:16
Awake, O north wind . . .

The bride speaks. The north wind is a cold wind. Perhaps you feel cold presently — you don't feel the intense love for Jesus that you would like to or once did; you feel distant and alone. That is the blowing of the north wind.

Let it blow — because the times which are devoid of tingly feelings or 'Holy Ghost goose bumps' provide glorious opportunity for you to demonstrate your love for the Lord through diligence in worship, prayer, and study of His Word — even though you don't feel His presence.

Folks, just because the feelings aren't there, it doesn't mean that the Lord has forsaken you. On the contrary, He is allowing you to go through seasons of coldness in order to grant you the privilege of learning to walk by faith and not by feeling.

Feelings are oh, so fickle. They're affected by what you ate last night, by what your family said to you this morning, by the media, the weather, the economic outlook. Not so with faith. It is a constant because it is totally independent of outside circumstances. Therefore, the Lord, wanting the best for His people, desires us to walk in the surety and stability of faith.

Can you, like the maiden, say, 'Lord, I'm willing to go through a week, or a month, or a year of the blowing north wind in order to give to you without expecting the sense of Your presence in return'? Can you say, 'Lord, if I can best demonstrate what You have done in my life through periods of coldness, so be it'?

I have a problem: Most of the time, whenever I give to God, I get so much back that I can't really call it giving at all! I start to worship and say, 'Lord, this is a sacrifice of praise to You,' when suddenly, finding myself flooded with feelings of joy, I think, 'This is no sacrifice at all. Am I doing this to give — or am I doing this to receive?'

But when I feel somewhat distant from the Lord, it's an opportunity for me to give and give and give without necessarily receiving anything in return.

If you're going through a cold spell today, if the north wind is howling — rejoice. You have a unique opportunity to minister to Jesus, to give to Him worship and adoration, praise and thanksgiving regardless of your feelings.

Song of Solomon 4:16
. . . and come, thou south . . .

The south wind is a hot, arid wind. Perhaps you are presently walking through days of difficulty and times of fiery trials. That is the blowing of the south wind.

Precious people, it's not when you're prospering and cruising through life that others can see Jesus in you. It's when they observe you walking through difficult days by the grace of God that they know He is real to you.

Song of Solomon 4:16
. . . blow upon my garden, that the spices thereof my flow out.

At Applegate Lake a few days ago, I was sitting on the grass when, all of a sudden, I smelled something. My mouth began to water and my stomach started to growl as the fragrance of barbequed steak worked its way down the hillside and into my nostrils.

Was it pleasing for the steak?
Probably not.

But it was indeed pleasing to me.

So too, when the winds of adversity, the winds of difficulty blow through our lives, a fragrance is released. It is either a foul odor of bitterness and hostility, jealousy and anger — or it is the sweet-smelling savour of praise and thanksgiving, worship and adoration.

You see, the wind itself does not determine what the fragrance will be. It merely releases the fragrance that is already present.

So when I find bitterness, anger, jealousy, or hostility coming forth — I've got to say, 'Father, it's not him or her or them or it. It's *me. I* smell. Father, forgive me. I thought I was farther along than that. Oh, Lord have mercy.'

What a beautiful way to live!

Folks, instead of saying,

> 'It's his fault', or
> 'They didn't understand,' or
> 'How come she's doing that?'

say,

> 'Oh, Lord, the fragrance in my life is not what it should be. I repent, Father. Change my heart,'

and you will find a pleasing fragrance emanating from your life.

Song of Solomon 4:16
Let my beloved come into his garden, and eat his pleasant fruits.

Take special note of this verse, saints, for in it is the key to life.

The key to life is saying: 'I'm Your garden, Lord. Eat of me. I exist for Your pleasure and Your glory. That is why I am alive today. That is why I will awake tomorrow. I exist for one reason: not to heap pleasure upon myself, not even to please others — but to please You.'

Why do you exist?
To bring pleasure to the Lord.

Tomorrow will be a fabulous, wonderful, exciting, fulfilling day if you'll say,

'Lord, I'm here to please You all day long. I'm taking You out for lunch. We'll go grab a burger, and I'm going to meditate on Your Word, talk to You, and worship You. Lord, on my coffee break, my thoughts and prayers are going to be ascending to Your throne. I'm going to carry a Scripture verse in my pocket that my thoughts might be upon You as I meditate upon it at various intervals of the day.'

The key is this: You exist to bring the Lord pleasure. You are His garden.

My Life: His Garden

A Topical Study of
Song of Solomon 4:12-5:1

THE Song of Solomon is a very wonderful and mystical book. Many people in reading it, see nothing more than an erotic, Oriental love song and a romantic piece of literature. In reality, however, it is much more than that, for it deals with the issue of marriage — particularly marriage between Jesus Christ our King and us, His Bride. And when it is read and studied in that context, it can be tremendously impacting and very encouraging.

Church, we are married to Jesus Christ. We are His Bride. Some people view their marriages as less than the best, strenuous and difficult. If you are in a situation today where you say, 'My marriage is not what I thought it would be or know it could be,' know this: Your marriage here is temporary and preparatory. That is, it is preparing you, tempering you, and training you for the Ultimate Marriage — that mystery of which Paul speaks in Ephesians 5 — when you will be linked to, loved by, and living with Jesus Christ forever.

> A garden enclosed is my sister, my spouse; a spring
> shut up, a fountain sealed.
>
> Song of Solomon 4:12

In the text before us, the king likens his bride to a garden, a lovely garden, an enclosed garden. In Solomon's day, every king had a well-tended, private garden outside of his palace where he could retire in the cool of the afternoon, the early part of the evening, and at the break of day. So, here this king, a type of Jesus Christ, looks at his bride who represents us and says, 'You're a garden to me — something sweet and precious, beautiful and enjoyable.'

I have a tendency to look at myself and say, 'A garden? Lord, I could understand it if You said I'm a parking lot, a city slum, or even a county dump. But Lord, You're calling me a *garden*?'

Listen, gang. Yes. You are His lovely garden. In Chapter 1, the maiden looked at herself and said, 'I am black, but comely.' She realized her blackness, her inadequacy, and yet she said, 'I'm comely.'

Why?
Because she was loved by the king.

I realize I too am black. I'm a sinner. I have all kinds of problems and all sorts of weaknesses. But, like the maiden, I can say today,

> 'I am black, but I am comely because Jesus Christ has brought me into His loving heart and life. He has chosen me as His personal garden.

> Why?

I don't know. It's a great mystery to me!'

Do you know what cracks me up, what tickles my heart, what makes me smile when I read through this book? Never once does the king say to his maiden,

'You're lovely, but maybe you should think about changing your hairstyle.'

'You're lovely, but you could lose a few pounds.'

'You're lovely, but I don't like the length of your nose.'

No, in *every* chapter, the king affirms his maiden.

Gang, listen. This Song is Jesus speaking to you personally. He's not saying, 'I'll love you if you get it together or if you try and do better.' He's saying, 'I'm in love with you right now.'

Most of us believe that Jesus loves us generically. He has to — after all, He's Jesus and He loves everybody. But that's not the message of this book. The message of this book is that He loves you individually and is in love with you radically.

Oh, that we might see ourselves that way, that we might see ourselves in Christ Jesus —
> washed by His blood,
>> sanctified by His Spirit,
>>> loved, *really loved* by Him.

In Rochester, New York, a couple of weeks ago, a retired army sergeant fatally shot a 70-year-old woman as she left Mother's Day services. He admitted that he mistook the woman for his estranged wife because he forgot his glasses. 'I'm sorry about the other woman. I meant to kill my wife,' Percy Washman told police.

Because he forgot his glasses, Percy didn't see the woman accurately and ended up murdering her tragically.

Folks, sometimes I forget my glasses. I look at people and say, 'They're out of it. She's out of it. He's out of it.' Or I look at myself and say, 'I'm out of it.' It's because I'm not seeing things accurately.

The Bible says that we are the righteousness of God because we are in Christ Jesus (II Corinthians 5:21). When I really see that, I will not shoot you indiscriminately or commit spiritual suicide personally. When I look through the glasses of Scripture, I see what Jesus Christ did on Calvary's Cross — that He took all the sin and junk we've committed, paid for it, and now says, 'Your sins and iniquities will I remember no more,' (Hebrews 8:12).

> Awake O north wind; and come, thou south;
> blow upon my garden, that the spices thereof
> may flow out.
>
> Song of Solomon 4:16

The bride is so blessed to be the garden of her beloved, that she invites the cold north wind and the hot south wind to blow through her life in order that spices might be released from her.

How can the sweetness of Jesus flow from you?
Through the fiery trials and troubles of the south wind.

You see, it's not when you're prospering and cruising that people can see Jesus in you. It's when the south wind — hot times, difficult days, seasons of struggle, times of tribulation — blows through your life that people will want to know how you stand up under the pressure.

It is when you can answer, 'It's only because of Jesus and His grace that I'm not collapsing or caving in,' that those around you will be drawn to Him. Truly His fragrance flows from you in the time of the south wind.

And in the time of the north wind — in those times you feel cold; when you don't feel the intense love for Jesus you would like to, or that you once did — His fragrance is released as well. For when you don't feel His touch or His presence, He's giving you the opportunity to learn to walk by faith.

Here's what I have found: When I don't feel the Lord's presence, I have learned to rejoice and say,

> 'Great! Lord, I can worship You today without getting back more than I've given. I can truly just give to You, Lord, because I don't feel Your presence today. You've chosen to allow the north wind to blow today, or this week, or this month.'

Folks, I've gone through *months* when I haven't felt the warm presence of the Lord. I have come to actually embrace those times and look forward to those periods when I can say,

> 'Lord, I thank You for this opportunity to worship You and to love You without getting more in return than I give.'

Today, if you're going through a cold spell, if the north wind is blowing — rejoice. You have opportunity to really minister to Jesus. Just give and give and give, regardless of how you feel.

> Let my beloved come into his garden,
> and eat his pleasant fruits.
>
> Song of Solomon 4:16

Folks, I ask you to underline this verse because within it lies the key to life.

Who is it Who does anything good within us? Who is it Who produces fruit for our lives?

It's Jesus.

Why does He produce those fruits?
For His enjoyment.

Saints, when you bring the Lord pleasure, you are fulfilling the very reason for your existence.

> In Matthew 21, Jesus walked by a fig tree which had a lot of leaves. Hungry, Jesus reached to pick from the tree, but found no fruit. Consequently, He cursed the tree, the roots immediately withered, and it died.

Why did Jesus do that?

He was showing us that a tree which does not please Him, will never be of any value to anyone else, including itself.

If your tree, your garden, your life, precious people, is not existing to please your Lord and your Creator, no matter how healthy you might seem outwardly, you are a cursed individual spiritually. You'll dry up from the roots and live out a meaningless existence.

Jesus wasn't being cruel when He cursed the tree, He was showing us something. If your life is not satisfying Him, it will be no good to anyone else — not even to yourself. *All* things were created by Him and *for* Him, Colossians 1 declares.

Live every day with your primary intent being to bring the Lord pleasure — to delight Him with praise and worship, to walk and talk with Him, to enjoy and receive His love — and watch your life produce abundant fruit for His satisfaction and for the nourishment of those around you.

> I am come into my garden, my sister, my spouse:
> I have gathered my myrrh with my spice; I
> have eaten my honeycomb with my honey; I
> have drunk my wine with my milk:
>
> Song of Solomon 5:1

When the bride invited her beloved to enjoy the garden he had cultivated within her, he said, 'I've come.'

But notice what else he said:

> Eat O friends; drink, yea, drink abundantly, O
> beloved.
>
> Song of Solomon 5:1

I say,

> 'Lord, come into my garden.
>> Today it will be just You and me.
>>> I come to the garden alone . . . .'

But guess what the Lord does.

He brings a whole bunch of other people with Him and says,

> 'Eat, O friends. Everybody feast on Jon.'

I say,

> 'Quit picking on me. Back away. Move. Get out of here.'

Yet the Lord continues to bring company with Him.

Why?

Because He's not only in love with me, but with a whole bunch of other people whom He's linking together as an eternal Bride. He wants us to get it together here, and love each other now — because we're going to be linked to each other and living with each other for the next quabillion years.

That is why Jesus said, 'All men shall know that you are My disciples by your love for each other,' (John 13:35). Herein you show that your love for the Lord is real: by loving your brother, your sister, and the people He brings into your garden.

Saints, read through this section again, and you will find it truly pregnant with meaning.

When Tammy was pregnant with Benny, she and Christy, who was seven years old at the time, were walking in from the store, their arms loaded with groceries. Tammy dropped something and reached down to pick it up.

Christy, aware of Tammy's condition said, 'No, mommy. Don't stoop down. Your stomach will burst!'

So too, if you'll stoop down and take a close look at the Song of Solomon this week — prayerfully, mystically, spiritually, personally, romantically — you'll burst!

You'll burst with blessing when you realize
> that Jesus is in love with you;
>> that you were created for Him;
>>> that He wants to come in and enjoy your life;
>>>> and that He wants to bring His friends with Him.

The Lord *loves* you, gang. What a glorious truth that is!

CHAPTER FIVE

THE Song of Solomon is a mystical, majestic allegory. It's the story of the love of a shepherd-king, great and glorious in wealth and might, for a woman who was previously impoverished, a woman who acknowledged her blackness.

The allegory is obvious: The shepherd-king is a picture of our Lord and Savior, Jesus Christ. He is the King of Kings. He is the Good Shepherd that laid down His life for His sheep. The maiden is a picture of His Bride, His Church — us.

We saw how the shepherd-king brought the maiden into his presence and took her to be his bride. They shared a night of intimacy and love together. The next morning, he was up early — skipping on the hills and leaping on the mountains. He stood outside her window and called out to her saying, 'Come! Rise! The birds are singing, the flowers are blooming. Let's get going!'

But his bride answered, 'You go ahead. I'll stay in bed until the dawn breaks — and I'll catch up with you later.' As you recall, she found out much to her dismay, that he didn't come home. When evening came, she went on a frantic search for him. When she found him, he didn't come down on her. In fact, the shepherd-king never has one single negative word to say about his bride because, you see, our King has not a single negative word to say about us, about you.

Why?

Because we are cleansed by His blood. We are hid in Christ Jesus. We are robed with His righteousness. Thus, He looks at us and sees, as Ephesians declares, a glorious church without spot or wrinkle (Ephesians 5:27).

Practically, we see all kinds of spots and a whole bunch of wrinkles. But positionally, the Lord sees us cleansed in His blood and robed in His righteousness.

Most believers have a tendency to believe that God is mad at them. Oh, they know He loves them, but they think He is also disgusted with them

> for not praying enough,
> > for not giving enough,
> > > for not ministering enough.

They fail to understand their position in Christ Jesus — that they are hid in Christ, that there is therefore now *no* condemnation to them that are in Christ Jesus (Romans 8:1).

I have news for you: God isn't mad at you. And that's what this book is really all about — to show you the way He looks at you. It's a fabulous day when the understanding that you are not condemned; that you are the righteousness of God in Christ Jesus (II Corinthians 5) really takes root in your theology.

Song of Solomon 5:1
I am come into my garden, my sister, my spouse: I have
gathered my myrrh with my spice; I have eaten my honeycomb
with my honey; I have drunk my wine with my milk . . .

The bride invited the king to come into the garden which he had cultivated within her — and he came.

So too, when we say, 'Lord, come into my garden,' He comes — but He doesn't come alone . . .

Song of Solomon 5:1
. . . eat O friends; drink, yea, drink abundantly, O beloved.

The bridegroom doesn't come alone — He brings a whole group of people with him. And that's the way it is with our Lord.

We say, 'Lord it's just You and me — sweetly talking and communing in the garden.' And guess what He does. He invites hundreds to trample on us, pick from us, and squash us.

We say, 'Wait a minute, Lord. I said *You* could come into my garden — not *them.'*

But the Lord says, 'When I come, I bring My friends with Me.'

That's why the Apostle John asked, 'How can you say you love God if you hate your brother?' (I John 4:20). It's hypocrisy. It's inconsistent to say, 'I love You, Lord — but I'm mad at my brother,' because the one you're mad at is His friend, His love.

Song of Solomon 5:2
I sleep, but my heart waketh: it is the voice of my beloved that knocketh, saying, Open to me, my sister, my love, my dove, my undefiled: for my head is filled with dew, and my locks with the drops of the night.

Verse two begins a new section and a new situation. The honeymoon is over. And the bridegroom was out all night.

That doesn't surprise me, for Jesus said, 'Foxes have holes and the birds have their nests, but the Son of Man has nowhere to lay His head,' (Matthew 8:20). John 7 ends with every man going to his house, but John 8:1 says Jesus went to the mountain. He had no home.

And here is the bridegroom, with dew in His hair, knocking on the door of his bride.

Song of Solomon 5:3
I have put off my coat; how shall I put it on? I have washed my feet; how shall I defile them?

'Oh, lord,' answers the bride, 'My coat is off. I'm relaxing presently. My feet have been washed. I've been cleansed previously.'

Isn't that like us?

The Lord knocks and we say,

> 'Oh, Lord, *Family Ties* just came on. *Newsweek* just arrived. My friend just called up. Oh, Lord, I just put off my coat. Surely You

can't be knocking *now*. You can't be desiring to spend time with me *now*, Lord.'

We are relaxing in the present, or we are relying on the past —

'Lord, my feet have been washed. I went to a foot-washing last Sunday night. Isn't that good enough for awhile, Lord? Surely I'm clean and right with You.'

How often the Lord calls us and woos us but we say,

'As soon as the ninth inning is over, I'll spend time on my knees, I'll get my Bible — but Lord, what a great game this is. Let's finish out the game and I'll see You, later.'

And then I find I miss the moment that the Lord was desiring to spend with me, to give understanding to me.

That's what happened to the bride. Again, she missed the moment.

Song of Solomon 5:4-5
My beloved put in his hand by the hole of the door, and my bowels [heart] were moved for him. I rose up to open to my beloved; and my hands dropped with myrrh, and my fingers with sweet smelling myrrh, upon the handles of the lock.

As the bride opens the door, she realizes the hand of her bridegroom had been upon the handle.

Song of Solomon 5:6
I opened to my beloved; but my beloved had withdrawn himself, and was gone: my soul failed when he spake: I sought him, but I could not find him; I called him, but he gave me no answer.

Please understand that there's a major difference between the first time the bride didn't respond to her shepherd-king and this time.

The first time she let him out of her sight was because of her ignorance. That is, he called to her, but she was ignorant of her need to respond immediately.

This time, it's because of her indifference. She now knows better and yet she's not willing to exert the energy to respond to his calling.

Perhaps some of you have missed the Lord in those special moments because of ignorance. Most of us, however, miss the Lord because of indifference. We're just too lazy to get out of bed, too preoccupied to respond.

And now we see her once again, longing for her love, realizing that the love she had shared only hours earlier had grown cold — which is exactly what happens to us when other things creep in and we no longer make time to respond to the Lord.

Song of Solomon 5:7
The watchmen that went about the city found me, they smote me, they wounded me; the keepers of the walls took away my veil from me.

As the bride searches for her bridegroom, what do the watchmen do?
They rail on her.

Sorry to say, that's what pastors and leaders often do. When, due to ignorance or indifference, people are separated from the Lord and from the intimacy and closeness they once shared with Him, so often it's the watchmen who figure it's their right to smite the Bride, to come down on the Bride, to expose the Bride.

Such watchmen are so much different than Jesus Christ,
> our
> > Coverer, Lover,
> > > Forgiver, Restorer,
> > > > Redeemer.

When Jesus ministered, it says the common people — people just like you — heard Him gladly and marveled at the gracious words He spake — blown away by His redemptive words, by His gracious teachings, by His love and forgiveness (Luke 4:22).

The Lord *loves* you, precious people. Remember this allegory the next time a watchman comes off the wall and starts to kick you around or beat you up.

Now, if there *needs* to be correction in our lives, how does it take place?

In Galatians 6:1, Paul wrote, 'Brethren if any be overtaken in a fault, you who are spiritual, restore such a one in the spirit of meekness, considering yourself lest you also be tempted.' A *true* watchman, a true shepherd, will restore a sister or a brother in need of correction with a meek spirit — desiring to see people redeemed and restored, not rebuked and rejected.

Why is it that we're hardest on those we love?

> Guys, think about it. If your wife comes home with a wrinkle in the front fender of the car, you say, 'Honey, why don't you watch where you're going? Come on, now. You *know* this is going to make our insurance rates go up. Couldn't you have been more careful?' And on and on we go.

> And yet, if a woman you don't even know hits your car, you say, 'Oh, that's OK. It's alright. I'm insured. It's no problem!' We're so gracious and loving and calm with people we don't know. But if it's our wife or our kids — we read them the riot act.

When someone comes down on you, beats up on you, and takes your veil from you, try to remember this: The reason they're so down on you is because they love you. If they didn't love you, they would be much nicer to you!

> **Song of Solomon 5:8-9**
> **I charge you, O daughters of Jerusalem, if ye find my beloved, that ye tell him, that I am sick of love. What is thy beloved more than another beloved, O thou fairest among women? what is thy beloved more than another beloved, that thou dost so charge us?**

'What's so special about this one you love?' ask the daughters of Jerusalem. 'Why do you seek him so fervently?'

Song of Solomon 5:10-16
My beloved is white and ruddy, the chiefest among ten thousand. His head is as the most fine gold, his locks are bushy, and black as a raven. His eyes are as the eyes of doves by the rivers of waters, washed with milk, and fitly set. His cheeks are as a bed of spices, as sweet flowers: his lips like lilies, dropping sweet smelling myrrh. His hands are as gold rings set with the beryl: his belly is as bright ivory overlaid with sapphires. His legs are as pillars of marble, set upon sockets of fine gold: his countenance is as Lebanon, excellent as the cedars. His mouth is most sweet: yea, he is altogether lovely.

As the bride speaks of her beloved, we see Jesus in a very powerful, beautiful way.

For a topical study of Song of Solomon 5:10-16,
entitled 'A Loving Look At Our Lovely Lord',
turn to page 69.

Song of Solomon 5:16
This is my beloved, and this is my friend, O daughters of Jerusalem.

Some married couples are passionately in love, but they fight like cats and dogs, and tell me they're not even friends. Romantically and physically they're in love — but they don't like each other very much.

Not so with Jesus. He's not only your Lover — He's also your Friend (John 15:15). And He desires to cultivate a deep and meaningful relationship with you.

If you spent as much time with your best friend as you spend with the Lord on a daily basis, how deep would your friendship be? If you spent four minutes a day, or five minutes every other day, or twenty minutes once every third week — what kind of friendship would you have?

So often we say, 'I just don't feel the presence of the Lord. I don't enjoy His company.' It's because we haven't invested in cultivating His friendship.

'Be not deceived,' warned Paul, 'Whatever a man sows, that shall he also reap,' (Galatians 1:12).

Jesus *enjoys* me. Even though many times I tire of and don't even like myself, He continues to call me friend.

What a great and marvelous mystery!

A LOVING LOOK AT OUR LOVELY LORD

A Topical Study of
Song of Solomon 5:10-16

A NEW sandwich is making its debut in sandwich shops and delicatessens across the nation: the Ollie North Hero Sandwich, composed of a full pound of all-American beef, a slight hint of Swiss cheese, lots and lots of shredded lettuce, and an ounce or two of ham.

Now, whether or not he is indeed a bona fide hero, all across America people are talking about Oliver North.

> One of his radical supporters was asked by a reporter, 'How can you call Oliver North a hero when he has admitted to lying to Congress and to our national leaders?'

> The young man answered, 'Well, Ollie North has many fine qualities. And nobody's perfect.'

His statement struck me. Here's a man saying, 'Ollie North is my hero. I see he's got some problems, but so what? Nobody's perfect.'

Folks, I have news for you today: Our Hero — Jesus Christ — is absolutely, totally, completely perfect —

no flaws,

no faults,

no failures.

I love that! The bride, speaking of her bridegroom said, 'He is altogether lovely,' (5:16). Indeed, there is *only* One who is altogether lovely.

When Isaiah, the prophet, saw the Lord high and lifted up, he said, 'Woe is me. I am undone.' Literally, 'I am un-together,' (Isaiah 6:5).

When Peter the Apostle saw the power of the Lord, he said, 'Depart from me. I am a sinful man,' (Luke 5:8).

When John the Revelator saw the greatness and the glory of the Lord, he fell down as a dead man (Revelation 1:17).

Every man, no matter how spiritual or holy he might seem, is in reality, flawed, imperfect, and undone.

But there is One Who is All Together — Jesus Christ.

As the bride began to think about and comment on the beauty of her shepherd-king, the daughters of Jerusalem said, 'What's so special about him?'

That is what the world asks us.

'What's so special about your Shepherd-King?'

'What's so special about your Bridegroom?'

'What's so special about this Jesus whom you worship?'

As you look at the bride's response, you will see it is the perfect answer for anyone who wants to know more about our lovely Lord.

My beloved is white . . .
Song of Solomon 5:10

As the bride describes her beloved, she first says, 'He is white.'

Whiteness speaks of Purity. How thankful I am that our Bridegroom, Jesus Christ, is so totally pure that even His enemies could find no fault in Him (John 18:38).

. . . and ruddy . . .
Song of Solomon 5:10

Ruddiness speaks of Vitality. The purity of Jesus is not unrelatable, or unlikable. He was known as the friend of sinners (Matthew 11:19). Street people hung around Him and sinners loved spending time with Him because there was a robustness, a vitality, a healthiness in His life that attracted people to Him.

This Jesus was no gentle Jesus meek and mild as is so often portrayed by those who don't know Him. Jesus was One Who, with eyes glowing and muscles bulging, walked through the Temple, overturning the tables of perhaps 100 men who dared not stand up to this single Individual (Mark 11:15-16).

Indeed there was a vitality about Jesus.

> . . . the chiefest among ten thousand.
> Song of Solomon 5:10

This speaks of His Superiority.

Thousands come on the scene and claim to have spiritual insight. Tens of thousands claim to have revelation. The gurus come and go and the Shirley MacLaines show up and make a splash for a few years, but there is One Who stands above and beyond, One Whose words are ageless, One Whose thoughts are impacting for all humanity, for all eternity. Jesus is the singular One among ten thousand.

> His head is as the most fine gold. . .
> Song of Solomon 5:11

Gold speaks of Deity. Not only does Jesus possess purity, vitality, and superiority — but also Divinity.

There are those who say, 'Jesus was just one of the enlightened masters. He never claimed to be God.'

Not so.

Jesus did indeed claim to be God when He said, 'I and my Father are one,' (John 10:30) — and so incensed were the people who heard such blasphemy, that they picked up rocks, ready to stone Him.

'In Him,' wrote the Apostle Paul, 'dwells all the fulness of the Godhead bodily (Colossians 2:9). Paul must have scratched his head as he went on to write, 'Great is the mystery of godliness — that God was manifest in the flesh,' (I Timothy 3:16).

All the fulness of God manifested in Jesus Christ?
What a mystery!

> There is a spider that lives in the Amazon Jungle basin who, the
> micro-second he jumps into water, blows a bubble around himself.
> As he begins to sink, he regulates the pressure of his bubble by
> allowing air in and out. Thus, he is able to hang out on the bottom
> of the Amazon River for up to two hours before he rises back to
> the surface, floats to shore, pops his bubble, and walks away.

Jesus Christ came from heaven to this planet with His Deity fully intact.
Encased by Divinity, He was not just a good moral man, but God Himself.
Thus He was able to live in this sinful world without being drowned by it.

> . . . his locks are bushy, and black as a raven.
> Song of Solomon 5:11

This speaks of Immutability.

Jesus never changes. He never gets older. His locks never get specks of gray.
The writer of Hebrews declares Jesus to be the same yesterday, today, and
forever (Hebrews 13:8). Jesus never gets old or tired or grumpy. James the
Apostle wrote that there is no shadow of turning in Him (James 1:17).

> Mary Elizabeth is ten months old. She has a monitor in her
> nursery so we can listen to her while she's sleeping. A couple of
> mornings ago, Mary woke up crying. Tammy turned to me and
> said, 'Oh, no. Mary's going to have a terrible day today. If she starts
> out on the wrong foot, it goes downhill from here.'

I'm so thankful we don't have to approach our Lord and say, 'Oh, no. It's going to be a hard day with Jesus. He's grumpy today.'

No, His locks are bushy. He stays young. He doesn't change.

> His eyes are as the eyes of doves by the rivers
> of waters, washed with milk, and fitly set.
> Song of Solomon 5:12

This speaks of Sympathy.

The eyes of Jesus are not eyes that condemn you, eyes that are suspicious of you, eyes that are watching to smash and destroy you when you get out of line. His eyes are those of a creature known for its gentleness, its peacefulness, its quietness. His eyes are doves' eyes.

In the courtyard of Caiphus, Peter warmed himself by the fire of the enemy as Jesus was being tried inside. Frustrated and fearful, Peter denied even knowing Jesus.

After Peter swore the third time that he had no part with Jesus, the cock crowed, the doors burst open, Jesus looked at Peter . . . and Peter wept (Matthew 26:75).

Why?

Jesus' look was not the look of condemnation, nor of accusation. Rather, with doves' eyes, He said, 'Peter, I told you this would happen. I understand your nature. I forgive your weakness.'

It was Jesus' look of compassion that broke Peter's heart.

So too, Jesus looks with doves' eyes

at we who have denied Him by not spending time with Him,

at we who have ignored Him or lived contrary to Him,

at we who have had a week where we haven't been what we should have been,

and He says to us, as He said to Peter,

'I forgive you. If you love Me, feed My sheep — keep going,' (John 21:15).

> His cheeks are as a bed of spices, as sweet flowers: his lips like lilies, dropping sweet smelling myrrh.
> Song of Solomon 5:13

His fragrance is Comely.

The average person emits thirty-six distinctive odors for a combination of 150 smells. Forensic pathologists are developing 'scent prints' whereby they can identify people by the smell they radiate.

The scent of Jesus Christ is like flowers. The more time we spend with Him, the closer we draw to Him, the more we find that His is a comely, attractive, beautiful fragrance indeed.

> His hands are as gold rings set with the beryl . . .
> Song of Solomon 5:14

The ring speaks of Authority, for it was with his ring that a ruler would stamp his seal upon official documents.

The disciples, marvelling as Jesus stilled the storm, said, 'We never saw such authority,' (Luke 8:25).

So too, according to His perfect plan for our lives, Jesus can speak to any wind that's blowing us away, or any storm that's beating us down — and it will be still. He has absolute authority to control every single aspect of our lives. There is nothing that can touch us, nothing that can come to us, nothing that can attack or effect us without His allowing it to be so. The moment He decides that a change is to be made or enough has come down, He will say, 'Be still,' — and it will. His hands are authoritative.

Forget Allstate. You're in good hands with Jesus Christ!

> . . . his belly is as bright ivory overlaid with sapphires.
>
> Song of Solomon 5:14

This speaks of Empathy.

In Solomon's day, it was the belly, not the heart, which was referred to as the seat of emotions. Taken from the tusks of dead elephants, ivory speaks emblematically of death.

Jesus, our Lord, our Savior, has been tempted or tested in all points — in every experience, with every kind of temptation or trial (Hebrews 4:15).

When He stood at the tomb of Lazarus and wept, He experienced death (John 11:35).

When they called Him one who was possessed with a devil and illegitimately born, He knew what it felt like to be misunderstood (Luke 11:15).

When He sat by the well, He knew what it was to be weary (John 4:6).

When He was sold out by one of His closest friends, He knew the feeling of betrayal (Matthew 26:50).

Are you tired today?
He can identify.

Are you tempted?
He understands.

Have you been put down recently?
He can relate.

His belly, the seat of His emotions, is as familiar with the pain of ivory as it is with the sparkle of sapphires.

> His legs are as pillars of marble, set upon sockets of fine gold . . .
>
> Song of Solomon 5:15

This speaks of Certainty.

There is a small box in the Library of Congress with a label on it that reads: 'The contents of the pockets of the President on the night of April 15, 1865.'

It contains:

> an initialled handkerchief,
> a country-boy's penknife,
> glasses and a case tied together with string,
> a small purse with five Confederate dollars,
> and several well-worn newspaper articles in which certain men
> called him one of the greatest leaders in American history.

Why did Abraham Lincoln carry those particular clippings?

Because at that time in his political career, he was in the midst of great controversy and tremendous pressure. Feeling the temptation to change positions on certain issues, perhaps he carried those clippings to confirm his sometimes faltering convictions, to steady his sometimes shaky persuasion.

Even the greatest leaders this world has known have faced moments of great uncertainty.

But when I look at Jesus Christ, I see One who set His face to go to Jerusalem — even though His disciples tried to avert Him, even though He knew it meant certain death (Luke 9:51).

His legs were marble set in sockets of gold.
> His face was set.
>> Nothing could deter Him
>>> from dying for you.

> . . . his countenance is as Lebanon, excellent
> as the cedars.
>> Song of Solomon 5:15

This speaks of Stability.

Jesus never gets 'down', but like a cedar of Lebanon — known for its towering height — He is solid, strong, and stable.

> His mouth is most sweet . . .
>> Song of Solomon 5:16

This speaks of Beauty.

Truly the mouth of Jesus is most sweet.

Luke wrote that the people wondered at the gracious words which proceeded out of His mouth (Luke 4:22).

Mark wrote that the common people heard Him gladly (Mark 12:37).

John wrote that the officers said, 'Never man spake like this man,' (John 7:46).

> . . . yea, he is altogether lovely.
>> Song of Solomon 5:16

After extolling the beauty of her beloved, the bride summed it all up by saying, 'He's all together.'

There is only One who is all together — Jesus Christ.

The more you study Him,
>the more you walk with Him,
>>the more you look at Him,
>>>the more you, too, will say,
>>>>'He is all together. He is altogether lovely.'

I believe the Lord has a simple word for us: We must take time to contemplate Jesus Christ. I've been reading in *Time* and *Newsweek* about recommended reading for the summer.

Could I recommend some reading?
Read one of the Gospels and consider Jesus Christ.

Study the personality,
>the characteristics,
>>the greatness
>>>of our Lord Jesus.

Perhaps it's been months or years since you've read a Gospel straight through and looked at the loveliness of your Lord. Consider doing so now.

If you do,
>you'll be elated,
>>delighted,
>>>and inspired

>as you get to know afresh this One Who is altogether lovely.

CHAPTER SIX

Song of Solomon 6:1
Whither is thy beloved gone, O thou fairest among women?
whither is thy beloved turned aside? that we may seek him
with thee.

IN Chapter 5, verse 9, the daughters of Jerusalem asked the bride what was so special about her beloved. After the bride described him in verses 10 through 16, here in Chapter 6, they say, 'We'll help you look for him. We want to find him, too.'

That's what happens whenever a congregation worships the Lord, extols His beauty, and talks about His characteristics. Praise and adoration cause the skeptics, the daughters of Jerusalem, to say, 'I want to know Him, too.'

I talked with a lady today who, claiming to be an agnostic, said, 'The interesting thing is, I enjoy coming to the Fellowship. I love seeing people who love the Lord. The worship and the genuine fellowship blow my mind.'

On the Day of Pentecost, 3,000 were saved. But what sparked the interest? What electrified the situation?

A group of 120 people were praising and worshipping God, speaking in other tongues and magnifying their Lord (Acts 2:1-7).

When people praise and worship, the daughters of Jerusalem invariably say, 'We want to seek Him too. We'll go with you.'

Song of Solomon 6:2-3
My beloved is gone down into his garden, to the beds of spices, to feed in the gardens, and to gather lilies. I am my beloved's and my beloved is mine: he feedeth among the lilies.

How did the bride suddenly know where to find her groom?

She worshipped him. She spoke of his characteristics. She extolled his virtues. She praised him.

Jesus said that the Father seeks those who will worship Him in spirit and in truth,' (John 4:23).

What does that mean?
It means that when you worship and extol the Lord, He'll find you.

How often this happens to me: I'll wonder where the Lord is. Then I'll take time to praise and honor Him. I'll think about His characteristics. I'll verbalize and articulate His glory and greatness — and suddenly, I'll experience His presence once again.

You see, the Father is seeking me when I worship Him — and I have found that it's a lot easier for the Lord to find me than for me to find Him!

The bride received revelation in the midst of worship — that is how she knew right where to find her shepherd-king.

Song of Solomon 6:4-7
Thou art beautiful, O my love, as Tirzah, comely as Jerusalem, terrible [awesome] as an army with banners. Turn away thine eyes from me, for they have overcome me: thy hair is as a flock of goats that appear from Gilead. Thy teeth are as a flock of sheep which go up from the washing, whereof every one beareth twins, and there is not one barren among them. As a piece of pomegranate are thy temples within thy locks.

Did the bridegroom say, 'Where were you, lady? How come you didn't open the door for me? I'm getting sick and tired of you. Why don't you pack your bags and move out?'

No.

He said, 'You're beautiful.'

Song of Solomon 6:8
There are threescore queens, and fourscore concubines, and virgins without number.

Here the king is saying, 'You're so comely. You're so beautiful. By the way, I've got sixty other queens, eighty concubines, and a whole bunch of virgins.'

That doesn't seem to fit here. I mean, why, in the middle of this beautiful romantic moment, would the king say, 'You ain't the only one'?

There's a reason: You see, sometimes we can think, 'Boy have we got it together. When we worship, there's just no church like ours. Aren't we so special to be so spiritual?'

And the Lord looks at us and says, 'You are lovely. I love you so deeply. But there are a whole bunch of other people I'm really in love with too.'

We have lists for everything: Best-selling Christian books, best-selling Christian records, best-selling Christian magazines. And somehow I think we think the Lord has a list of churches: Great churches, OK churches, barely passable churches — and on down.

Folks, that's not the way it is. The Lord is working with *all* fellowships — drawing out the best in them, and convicting and adjusting areas that are wrong. He has *many* people in *many* places with whom He's very much in love.

Song of Solomon 6:9
My dove, my undefiled is but one . . .

'Wait a minute,' you say. 'In verse 8, the king said he had sixty queens and eighty concubines; yet here in verse 9, he says, 'My dove is *one.*'

Is the king schizophrenic?
No.

His is the voice of our King, Jesus Christ, saying that He views His Church as a *united* Body, a *single* Bride.

Song of Solomon 6:9-10
. . . she is the only one of her mother, she is the choice one of her that bare her. The daughters saw her, and blessed her; yea, the queens and the concubines, and they praised her. Who is she that looketh forth as the morning, fair as the moon, clear as the sun, and terrible [awesome] as an army with banners?

The king extols the glory of his bride, just as Jesus is blown-away and blessed by the four-fold glory of His church.

For a topical study of Song of Solomon 6:10,
entitled 'The Glory Of The Church',
turn to page 89.

Song of Solomon 6:11
I went down into the garden of nuts to see the fruits of the valley . . .

The bride speaks, saying she went to the garden of nuts. That would be a great name for our church — Garden of Nuts Christian Fellowship. There's possibility there!

Song of Solomon 6:11-12
. . . and to see whether the vine flourished, and the
pomegranates budded. Or ever I was aware, my soul made me
like the chariots of Amminadib.

As she went to the garden, the bride found herself caught up in the
presence of her shepherd-king. She says, 'It was like chariots carrying me
away into glory.'

Song of Solomon 6:13
Return, return, O Shulamite; return, return, that we may look
upon thee.

When Peter, James, and John were on the Mount of Transfiguration with
Jesus, Peter said, 'Lord, it's good for us to be here. Let's build three booths
and camp out up here,' (Matthew 17:4). But the Lord knew that they had to
go back down the mountain because there were people below who needed
to be ministered to and healed.

Sometimes we say, 'I just want to stay caught up in Afterglows, Bible
studies and home group meetings,' — yet there's a company saying,

'Return, return. We need to be touched and taught, witnessed to,
prayed for, and loved. Will you do it, Church?

Will you come off the mountain? Will you leave the glory for a
moment to come and help us practically?'

Song of Solomon 6:13
What will ye see in the Shulamite? As it were the company of two armies.

In Genesis 32, Jacob named the place where he had done battle with the Lord, 'mahanaim,' meaning, 'two armies.' You see, previously, he had travelled with his family and entourage as a single army, but as he did battle with the Lord and really got to know Him, he realized that there had been a second army travelling with him all along — a supernatural army.

Folks, we are two congregations. Our friends and family sit beside us, but there's a second army also among us: A whole bunch of angels, who, according to Scripture, join with us (I Peter 1:12, I Corinthians 11:10) — studying us and trying to understand the incredible grace of a God Who would choose sinners like you and me.

NOTES

THE GLORY OF THE CHURCH

A Topical Study of
Song of Solomon 6:10

COMING home from a wedding last night, I picked up a hitchhiker named Eric. As we drove into town, I said, 'Cruise on out to the Fellowship sometime. I think you'll really be blessed.'

'Are you one of the teachers out there?' he asked.

'I'm the pastor,' I answered.

Then he really caught me off guard when he said, 'Oh? Well how do you like the Church Business?'

'Well, I'm not really into the 'Church Business,' I said. 'I'm very aware right now of the controversy concerning televangelism and peoples' image of the Church. I'm more into relationship. Our Fellowship is just really casual, and people kind of come as they are to worship and study the Scriptures' — which was kind of ironic, since I was dressed in a suit and tie with a boutonniere on my lapel.

Although for the next five minutes, I apologized for what people think of the Church, after I let him off, I was haunted in my heart about what I had said. As I drove home, the Lord continued to stir and speak to me as He brought to my mind a verse wherein the writer to the Hebrews declares, 'For both he that sanctifieth and they who are sanctified are all of one: for which cause he is not ashamed to call them brethren, Saying, I will declare thy name unto my brethren, in the midst of the church will I sing praise unto thee,' (Hebrews 2:11-12).

You see, even though we might feel the need to be defensive and apologetic about the Church, Jesus says specifically that He is not ashamed to call us brothers. That is why I am having such a wonderful time studying and meditating on the Song of Solomon — for in this book we see our Shepherd-King, Jesus Christ, talking to His maiden, His Bride, His Church — loving her, uplifting her, encouraging her.

Never once in the Song of Solomon does the shepherd-king have anything negative to say about his bride. The same is true of Jesus. He's not ashamed *of* us — He's in love *with* us!

In the passage before us, I would like you to note four qualities which illuminate the glories of the Bride of Christ, His Church.

> Who is she that looketh forth as the morning,
> fair as the moon, clear as the sun, and terrible
> as an army with banners?
>
> Song of Solomon 6:10

Perspective on life

Who is she that looketh forth as the morning . . .

The prophet Jeremiah said, 'It is of the Lord's mercies that we are not consumed, because his compassions fail not. They are new every morning,' (Lamentations 3:23). How I need morning to come as often as it does because in a 24-hour period, I've messed things up so royally that I *need* new mercies and a fresh start!

It is said that ignorance is bliss. Indeed that's true, for the more we know, the more we realize how tenuous everything is . . .

Wall Street is currently enjoying a bull run, but that can reverse very quickly unless the deficit gets under control.

This week we will fly our flag over Kuwaiti tankers in the Gulf.

Gas is creeping back up to a dollar a gallon.

We are now almost twice as dependent upon foreign oil as we were during the oil crisis of the 70's.

Yet we as the Church can look at the events that surround us personally and threaten us politically not with panic, frustration, or fear, but rather with understanding and perspective, saying, 'These are all signs of the times. Jesus told us they are signs of His return.'

The Church alone can face life with expectancy, with enthusiasm, with hope.

Two nights ago, I spent the evening with a young couple in their mid-twenties who love the Lord deeply. Two and a half weeks ago, the woman noticed her stomach protruding quite radically. She went to the doctor, and discovered it was cancer.

She and her husband shared with me that when they walked out of the doctor's office and into the hall, they looked at each other and began to laugh — not a laugh of cynicism, nor a laugh of escapism — but a laugh of true joy and thanksgiving that the Lord was in control of their situation, a laugh that said they were not going to succumb to the dread and fear of the medical profession.

What a joy to be with people who — even though they are inflicted with a situation that would drive others to drink or drugs, depression or divorce — live out the reality of Jesus Christ.

It is so exciting to be around people who are not full of gloom and doom, around people who say,

'God is the Source of my strength and health. He is on the throne and in control of the destiny of my life. I will trust in Him. I will look to Him and believe that everything that's happening to me is according to Divine design.'

Only in the Church do you find people who can look difficulty right in the eye and say,

'Through Christ Jesus we are more than conquerors,' (Romans 8:37).

Only the Church has an eternal perspective on life.

Purpose for life

. . . fair as the moon . . .

Jesus said, '*I* am the light of the world,' (John 8:12), and yet He also said to us, '*Ye* are the light of the world,' (Matthew 5:14).

How can that be?

It is not that we have light in and of ourselves. Rather, like the moon, we are those who reflect *His* love and *His* light to a world that is dark, doomed, and dying.

Your neighbors, your colleagues, your friends and your family — don't know Jesus if they're not a part of His kingdom. Thus, they can no more see the light of the Son in their darkened world than we can see sunlight at night. But, they *can* see the moon — the Church — reflecting His light.

As you know, the moon goes through different phases: half-moon, crescent moon, and is sometimes absent altogether.

Why?

Because to the extent that planet earth comes between the moon and the sun, the light of the moon diminishes.

So too with us. Our light will be diminished to the extent that we allow the world to get between us and the Son. Conversely, our light will shine to the degree that we remain in fellowship with Him.

The result?

If we are in close fellowship with the Son, not only will we light the darkness of others, but our own lives will be illuminated in the process.

When I witness, you know what happens? *I* am tremendously fulfilled.

When I pray for people who are hurting, *I* am encouraged.

When I share the Gospel, *my* faith soars.

When I share Scripture with another believer, *my* knowledge of Jesus increases exponentially.

Truly, the Church has been gifted with an incredible purpose for life.

Purity through life

. . . clear as the sun . . .

In the world's eyes, we are simply the moon, reflecting the glory of the Lord. But in the Lord's eyes, we are as bright as the sun. That is, He sees us linked with Him, actually a part of Him. One of the marvelous mysteries of marriage is that two become one. Thus, as His Bride, in the Lord's perspective we are as clear and as bright as He is.

What does that mean?

It means that my life is slowly but surely being purified by the heat of the Son. You see, just as the sun burns up over a million tons of mass every second, the Son burns the massive amount of junk in my life in order that His light might go forth.

This life is only preparatory, saints. The Lord is readying us and burning out the dross within us because we are one with Him and shall reign beside Him forever. Therefore, in this life, He purifies us through experiences that seem hot and heavy.

Mary Elizabeth has recently discovered the bowl of Reese's Peanut Butter Cups that sits on our coffee table. At ten months of age, not only is she old enough to figure out how to get her hand into the forbidden bowl — she's also old enough to understand the meaning of the word, 'No'.

So when Mary pulls herself up to the coffee table and reaches for the peanut butter cups, we say, 'No.' Then she gets a big smile on her face, looks right at us, and puts her hand into the bowl. We again say, 'No,' and slap her hand. She sits down and cries for awhile before pulling herself back up, smiling bigger than ever, and reaching for the bowl again.

How much like us! To justify our own desires, we smile sweetly and say,

'It's OK if I do this, isn't it, Father?'

And then we feel His love slap our hand.

Do you ever wonder why your hand gets slapped so often?
It's because the Bible says the Lord chastens those He loves (Hebrews 12:6).

When we, like Mary, reach for those things He knows are harmful to us, He says, 'No,' and chastens us in order to protect and purify those He loves.

Power in life

. . . and terrible [awesome] as an army with banners?

The Church is an awesome army whose purpose is to storm the gates of hell. We have a calling to invade the kingdom of darkness and death and see people rescued and brought into the Kingdom of life and love.

Thursday afternoon at 4:30, I was sitting in my office when I felt something very chilling. As I looked outside, I saw all of the sprinklers were on — which I didn't think unusual until one of our groundskeepers came running in, saying, 'Who turned on the sprinklers?'

At that moment, I looked outside and saw a gal walking by my office window with her arms up in the air, as if she were a bird. As she walked in the door, all of the electricity in the offices went off. The rooms went black. The computers went down. The praise music stopped. A moment later, the electricity came back on, but the praise music would not come back on over the system for the duration of her visit.

As she stood in the hallway, she started shrieking and yelling, saying she was a child of Abba, and that she was there to get help. While several of us watched, we saw her face go into strange contortions, and heard her speak with a deep and unforgettable voice.

Realizing we had a problem on our hands, we took her into the office and asked her what was going on. She said that she had come to save and water the world. But as her voice began to take on various tones, and as she alternately cursed and cried, the Lord spoke to my heart saying, 'Tell her to renounce the spirit of water.'

Now, I'm not given over to freaky stories of Satan. On the contrary, I feel that the Church today has more problems with demon obsession than demon possession. But, in obedience to the Lord, I said to her, 'You must, in the name of Jesus, renounce the spirit of water immediately, to which she replied, 'I will never renounce the spirit of water.'

At that moment, the story of the boy who tried to kill himself by drowning himself (Mark 9:17-27), flashed across my mind. So I said, 'There's a demon that is possessing and controlling you. You must renounce him and acknowledge that Jesus alone is Lord.'

'The spirit of water is Jesus,' she said, as she took a drink from the cup of water she carried. 'I'm thirsty.'

'Jesus is the Living Water,' I said. 'And whoever drinks of Him shall never thirst again. The water you're drinking of is a counterfeit water. Satan, a demon, is impersonating the living water which you desire.'

With that, she cursed and said, 'I will never renounce the spirit of water.'

Here was a girl who, according to her friend, had been in and out of mental institutions for the past eleven years. She came to the Fellowship; bizarre things happened; the Holy Spirit identified the problem — but she wouldn't respond. She chose instead to remain in service to Satan. I continue to pray for her because I believe at that moment there was a direct confrontation and a direct opportunity for liberation.

In world history, mankind has gone to two extremes. In previous ages, everything was superstitiously attributed to Satan and demons. In our present age, everything is attributed to psychological and mental problems.

But Satan is still real, gang. So are demons. And people are in all types of bondage as a result.

> The spirit of suicide sweeping our country is not because parents are not involved with their kids.

> It is not because music has suddenly become too heavy.

> It is because there is a demonic spirit that is out to destroy our youth.

We must recognize it.
> Mark's gospel teaches it.
> > Jesus dealt with it.

We are not told in the gospels that psychiatry is the answer. We are told that the Church must be engaged in spiritual warfare if we are to see people set free.

Folks, it's time we wake up and realize that there are some heavy things happening around us that cannot be cured by psychological counselling.

The answer is spiritual warfare:

Prayer,
Fasting,
Pleading the blood,
Speaking out the Word of God authoritatively.

We wrestle not against flesh and blood but against principalities and powers (Ephesians 6:12). Please don't be deceived, Church. Realize that there is a very real enemy who is seeking to destroy us.

Read the Gospels. Read the Book of Acts, and you'll see that when spiritual warfare took place, victory was the result. We are an awesome army, gang — marching under His banner.

What is His banner?

'He brought me to his banqueting table and his banner over me is love,' said the maiden (Song of Solomon 2:4).

The banner that flies over our heads is
        not the banner of militancy,
                not the banner of judgmental morality,
                        not the banner of confronting and condemning society.

It's the banner of love.

It's saying to people,
        'The Lord loves you,
                died in your place to pay the price of your sin,
                        and has beautiful plans for your future.
                        You're *loved* by Him!'

Gang, we, the Church of Jesus Christ, have been gifted with
> perspective *on* life,
>> purpose *for* life,
>>> purity *through* life,
>>>> and power *in* life.

If I see Eric, my hitchhiking friend again, I owe him an explanation. For I have been reminded once again that I am proud to be a part of the Church.

I really am.

Chapter Seven

Song of Solomon 7:1
How beautiful are thy feet with shoes, O prince's daughter . . .

THE king compliments his bride upon the beauty of her feet, which is somewhat unusual since feet are not necessarily the prettiest part of a person.

But therein lies an interesting thought. You see, according to Ephesians 6:15, we are shod with the preparation of the gospel of peace. That is, we stand on the gospel of peace — not upon our own efforts, works, or righteousness, but on the good news of God's peace with us.

When Moses stood on holy ground, what did God instruct him to do?
Remove the sandals *from* his feet (Exodus 3:5).

When the Prodigal returned home, what did his father do?
He put sandals *on* his feet (Luke 15:22).

Why?

Because Moses speaks of the Law, while the Prodigal speaks of grace.

If you think you can stand on the Law, forget it — take off your shoes. You'll never make it. You cannot earn or deserve God's blessings.

But if you're at a place where you say, 'I need God's forgiveness, grace, and mercy in my life,' then, like the Prodigal, you will experience the gospel of peace being placed upon your feet.

Dear Church, dear Bride, hear this: We do not stand on what we do or how we behave. We stand on the finished work of the Cross. We stand on what Jesus Christ has done for us. We stand on the gospel of peace.

Song of Solomon 7:1
. . . the joints of thy thighs are like jewels, the work of the hands of a cunning workman.

The muscle structure of the thighs is the strongest muscle structure in the entire body. It guards a woman's purity. Here we see the bride being loved and commended for her purity.

Song of Solomon 7:2
Thy navel is like a round goblet, which wanteth not liquor . . .

The navel speaks of independence. Whereas once we were tied to the world's system, we have now been freed by the Spirit of God. No longer are we in bondage to the world.

Song of Solomon 7:2
. . . thy belly is like an heap of wheat set about with lilies.

I find it interesting that throughout the Old Testament, Israel is likened to trees — a fig tree, an olive tree, a cedar of Lebanon — standing strong, unshakeable and immovable.

But here, the bride, the Church, is likened to wheat. I am personally very concerned about the Church feeling as though she's a tree — planted firmly, rooted deeply in the world; that she's been called to change the world system politically, governmentally, and economically.

Jesus said, 'My Kingdom is *not* of this world,' (John 18:36). We're not the tree, folks. We're wheat — meant to be cut down, carried away, and taken off to the King's barns and granaries.

Song of Solomon 7:3-4
Thy two breasts are like two young roes that are twins. Thy neck is as a tower of ivory; thine eyes like the fishpools in Heshbon, by the gate of Bath-rabbim: thy nose is as the tower of Lebanon which looketh toward Damascus.

The Book of Leviticus states that if a man had a flat nose, he could not serve in the priesthood (Leviticus 21:18). I believe that stipulation symbolically says that those who are effective in service cannot be seduced or tricked by every false wind of doctrine or every theological fad that comes their way. Rather, they must have a developed spiritual sense of smell in order to discern things that are amiss.

Song of Solomon 7:5
Thine head upon thee is like Carmel, and the hair of thine head like purple; the king is held in the galleries.

I Corinthians 11 teaches that the hair speaks of submission. Purple is the color of royalty. Purple hair, therefore, typifies one who is submitted to the authority of the king.

Song of Solomon 7:6-9
How fair and how pleasant art thou, O love, for delights! This thy stature is like to a palm tree, and thy breasts to clusters of grapes.

The palm tree is the only tree that gets more fruitful as it gets older. Although you might be getting up in years, your usefulness or fruitfulness need not diminish.

On the contrary, you who are older are to be as a palm tree: increasing in wisdom, more powerful and prevailing in prayer, more stable in your walk in the Spirit.

Song of Solomon 7:10
I said I will go up to the palm tree, I will take hold of the boughs thereof: now also thy breasts shall be as clusters of the vine, and the smell of thy nose like apples; and the roof of thy mouth like the best wine for my beloved, that goeth down sweetly, causing the lips of those that are asleep to speak.

Meditate on this passage, for there are wonderful truths tucked away within it that speak of how Jesus looks at *you*.

Song of Solomon 7:10
I am my beloved's, and his desire is toward me.

Notice how the bride is maturing:

In Chapter 2, she said, 'My beloved is mine,' (2:16).
In Chapter 6, she said, 'I am my beloved's and my beloved is mine,' (6:3).
Here in Chapter 7, she says, 'I am my beloved's.'

'I am my beloved's — period,' said the bride. 'I'm not trying to claim him. I'm not trying to manipulate him.'

There comes a time in your walk when you're no longer trying to manipulate God. May the broadcasters on Christian TV — with their gold rings and Cadillacs — understand this truth.

Certain shows on Christian TV grieve many of our hearts as they try to force God to do their bidding. Theirs is a wrong theology. It's not Biblical. It's not Christ-like. It's not right. Be aware of it. Stay away from it. Don't get sucked into it. May God give you a nose like the tower of Lebanon!

It grieves my heart that the Church is being told to make demands of God as if He were our genie in a bottle. He's God and we are His servants — not the other way around.

Whereas before the bride said, 'My beloved is mine,' now she's saying, 'I'm my beloved's.' What a sweetening and softening of her walk.

Song of Solomon 7:11-13
Come, my beloved, let us go forth into the field; let us lodge in the villages. Let us get up early to the vineyards; let us see if the vine flourish, whether the tender grape appear, and the pomegranates bud forth: there will I give thee my loves. The mandrakes give a smell, and at our gates are all manner of pleasant fruits, new and old, which I have laid up for thee, O my beloved.

In Chapter 1, the bride despised the fields. Here in Chapter 7, she wants the king to go back with her to the fields. What made the difference?

> When the demoniac of Gadara was delivered by Jesus, he said, 'Lord, I want to follow You wherever you go.' But Jesus said, 'Go back to where you came from — that your family and friends might see the glorious work of God,' (Mark 5:1-19).

There are times when we think it would be wonderful to follow Jesus to Mexico, to Honduras, to Brazil, or Tahiti — but there comes a point in your maturity when you say instead,

> 'I'm ready to go talk to the guys I used to drink with and tell them about Jesus.'

'I'm ready to pour my heart out to my parents and explain to them that Jesus loves them.'

'I'm ready to go back to where I came from.'

I'm not discounting being sent out, but there's also an important place when, in your maturity, you realize that mission fields are around you on every side. The old missionary saying is true: There's no sense going across the ocean if you won't go across the street.

Have you gone across the street? Is your neighborhood being affected? Is your workplace changing in atmosphere because you're there witnessing, praying, loving, encouraging, and sharing? The toughest place to minister is at home. That's why Jesus said, 'A prophet is not without honor except in his own country,' (Matthew 13:57).

And that's why the bride showed great maturity when she said to her king, 'I'm ready to go back home — and to take you with me.'

NOTES

CHAPTER EIGHT

Song of Solomon 8:1-4
O that thou wert as my brother, that sucked the breasts of my mother! when I should find thee without, I would kiss thee; yea, I should not be despised. I would lead thee, and bring thee into my mother's house, who would instruct me: I would cause thee to drink of spiced wine of the juice of my pomegranate. His left hand should be under my head, and his right hand should embrace me. I charge you, O daughters of Jerusalem, that ye stir not up, nor awake my love, until he please.

IN Solomon's culture, it was acceptable to publicly kiss a family member, but taboo to kiss one's spouse. Thus, the bride says to her king, 'I wish you were my brother, so I could freely express my feelings for you.'

Like the Shulamite bride, I find myself limited in loving my Lord because I 'see through a glass darkly'. While I am completely impressed with what I do see, I'm so aware of how much I don't see.

But guess what. Soon there will be no more limitations. 'For now we see through a glass darkly, but then shall we see Him face to face,' (I Corinthians 13:12).

Song of Solomon 8:5
Who is this that cometh up from the wilderness, leaning upon her beloved?

This question, asked by the daughters of Jerusalem, is pregnant with meaning. 'Who is it that comes out of the wilderness leaning upon her beloved?'

It's us.

We are delivered from the wilderness of this world by leaning upon our Beloved — Jesus Christ.

Song of Solomon 8:5
I raised thee up under the apple tree: there thy mother brought thee forth: there she brought thee forth that bare thee.

The king's statement is a difficult one to understand, yet I believe the application is that Jesus is not only our Lover and our Friend — He's also the One Who brought us forth. He's our Creator and our Everlasting Father (Isaiah 9:6).

Song of Solomon 8:6
Set me as a seal upon thine heart, as a seal upon thine arm: for love is strong as death; jealousy is cruel as the grave: the coals thereof are coals of fire, which hath a most vehement flame.

'Challenges are coming,' says the bride. 'There will be difficulties in our relationship. So seal me upon your heart and upon your arm.'

The High Priest carried the names of the tribes of Israel on his breastplate and upon his shoulders (Exodus 28:12, 29). So too, Jesus Christ, our Great High Priest, has us on His heart and on His shoulders. The heart speaks of His tenderness towards us, and the shoulders of His strength surrounding us.

Song of Solomon 8:7
Many waters cannot quench love, neither can the floods drown it: if a man would give all the substance of his house for love, it would utterly be condemned.

'Love will persevere,' says the bride. 'But if a person tries to buy love, it will be condemned.'

Church, rejoice in the fact that the Lord has you on His heart and upon His shoulders. Challenges will come in your relationship, but love will overcome. And yet if you try and buy His love, that love will be condemned.

Don't try and buy the Lord's love. Don't say,

> 'The Lord must really love me today because I had devotions for an hour. What a day this is going to be! I really earned God's love today.'

That kind of love is useless because it is based upon your works instead of God's grace.

'Then why have devotions?' you ask.

Because I love my Lord and I want to spend time with Him. I gain strength in His presence and receive understanding. But I'm not trying to prove or earn a greater love.

Did you know that if you had devotions every day this week for seven hours the Lord would not love you any more than if you didn't have devotions at all?

Now, if you have devotions for seven hours, there will inevitably be a glow on your face and strength in your heart. *You* will be changed — but His love for you will not be affected because His love for you is not based upon your actions. It is based solely upon His own nature. That is why Paul wrote that *nothing* shall separate us from the love of God in Christ Jesus (Romans 8:38-39).

Don't work for God's love.
Don't try to deserve it.
Just enjoy it!

Song of Solomon 8:8
We have a little sister, and she hath no breasts: what shall we do for our sister in the day when she shall be spoken for?

The bride is concerned about her little sister.

So too, as you grow in the Lord you will find yourself concerned about others.

Song of Solomon 8:9-10
If she be a wall, we will build upon her a palace of silver: and if she be a door, we will inclose her with boards of cedar. I am a wall and my breasts like towers: then was I in his eyes as one that found favour.

'If she's a wall, that is, separated — she'll live in a palace. But if she's a door, letting anyone and anything in — she'll be imprisoned.'

What is God saying to you and me?

When we say, 'Lord, we care about this person, this friend, this neighbor,' He says,

> 'If he's a door — open to everything, he'll be imprisoned forever. He's damned.

> But if he's a wall, if he wants to be right and to be separated from the things and the crud of this world, a palace will be his. He'll be saved and taken to heaven.'

This is a favorite text of those who are Arminian in theology, which places a great emphasis upon an individual's choice in his eternal destiny.

> **Song of Solomon 8:11**
> **Solomon had a vineyard at Baal-hamon; he let out the vineyard unto keepers; every one for the fruit thereof was to bring a thousand pieces of silver.**

Those who used the king's property were required to pay rent.

> **Song of Solomon 8:12**
> **My vineyard, which is mine, is before me: thou, O Solomon, must have a thousand, and those that keep the fruit thereof two hundred.**

The bride is not *required* to give. She *desires* to give.

So too, those who live under the Law are required: 'You must do this. You must do the other. You can't do that. You mustn't do that.' That's the Law.

But those who live in love say, 'Lord, I *desire* to give myself to You.'

The Law says, 'Responsibility!'
Love says, 'Respond.'

> **Song of Solomon 8:13**
> **Thou that dwellest in the gardens, the companions hearken to thy voice: cause me to hear it.**

'I want to hear your voice,' says the bride to her shepherd-king.

Jesus, our Good Shepherd said, 'My sheep hear My voice,' (John 10:27).

Song of Solomon 8:14
Make haste, my beloved, and be thou like to a roe or to a young hart upon the mountains of spices.

'Make haste,' said the beloved of the king —
    even as John, the beloved apostle said,
        'Come quickly, Lord Jesus,' (Revelation 22:20) —
    even as we His Bride say,
        'Come soon, Lord. We need You.'

_____

NOTES

So ends our study of the Song of Solomon. In reality, however, it has been merely an introduction. For the Song of Solomon is a book unlocked only through time and personal meditation.

Whenever you feel like the Lord doesn't love you, camp out for awhile in Romans 5-8. Then turn to the Song of Solomon. Mix Romans with Solomon — theology with mysticism — and you'll have the strength of two armies (6:13).

May the Lord bless you.
May you know that His love for you is constant and unconditional.
May you understand that you are now and forevermore
His Beloved Bride.